Newman's Spiritual Themes

E O' Gorman

C. S. Dessain

Newman's Spiritual Themes

Veritas Publications Dublin 1977

Sole distributors in U.K. (excluding Northern Ireland)
Fowler Wright Books Limited,
Tenbury Wells, Worcs., England, Tele: (08867) 286.

First published 1977 by
Veritas Publications,
Pranstown House, Booterstown Avenue, Co. Dublin.

Set in 11/12 Baskerville and
printed and bound in the Republic of Ireland by
Cahill (1976) Limited, Dublin.
Typography by Liam Miller.
Cover by Steven Hope.

Acknowledgements: for part of chapter 1, originally published as "Cardinal Newman and eternal punishment," Max Seckler (Hrsg.), *Begegnung,* 1972 Styria Graz Wien Koln; for chapter 3, originally published, in large part, as "Cardinal Newman and the eastern tradition" in *The Downside Review;* for chapter 4, originally published, in large part, as "Cardinal Newman and the doctrine of uncreated grace" in *The Clergy Review;* gratitude.

Nihil obstat:
Richard Sherry, D.D.
Censor, Deputatus.

Imprimatur
✠ Dermot,
Archbishop of Dublin.
31 January, 1977

ISBN 0-905092-26-0
Cat. No. 3348

Contents

Foreword

In the days of large folio volumes, there often appeared a small book alongside the vast tomes, which gave the gist of the matter in a handy and compact form. A favourite Latin title for this kind of companion volume was *Medulla Doctrinae,* the "marrow of the author's doctrine". The small book provided the real taste of what was in the larger tomes, and whetted the appetite for more.

Father Stephen Dessain was admirably fitted to perform such a service for the general reader with regard to Newman. In addition to his prodigious output in editing Volumes XI-XXX of Newman's *Letters and Diaries,* he had assimilated Newman's spiritual teaching to a remarkable degree, and had done much to spread it, particularly in his many published articles. The fruit of all this labour is culled here in this book in a pleasing and convincing form.

Originally intended as the basis of a retreat to be preached to the Oratory of France, it was in fact not delivered because of Father Stephen's sudden death scarcely a week before the retreat was due to begin.

The typescript of the conferences is presented here in the form in which Father Stephen left it. The numerous extracts from Newman have all been verified, and the quotations from sources other than Newman have been checked. Mr Gerard Tracey of Birmingham gave invaluable help in this part of the work.

Though an Englishman to his fingertips, Father Stephen had a few French phrases he was fond of repeating. One of them was: *faire valoir Newman.* A good

French dictionary gives as example of this turn of phrase, "a setting that shows off a precious stone". This book is such a setting.

Placid Murray, OSB
Glenstal Abbey
15 January 1977

1 Seeking the elusive truth

What is the special value of Cardinal Newman today? Various answers might be given. The fundamental one is that the effectiveness of the Christian religion, its power of controlling and influencing our lives, in the way God intends that it should, depends on the fullness and correctness with which it is held. Our Lord came "full of grace and truth", and "of his fullness we have all received", but at different times and places this life-giving truth has been impoverished, watered down, or else one or other aspect unduly emphasised. This can happen even in the Catholic Church, although it is protected from going astray in any fundamental way. In the Catholic Church since the Second Vatican Council there has been a generous effort to correct wrong emphases and to fill in omissions in the way we held or practised our Christian faith. When the Revealed Message is altered or exaggerated, it presents a caricature of its true self, thus failing to be effective, and deterring those who should be attracted to it.

In Newman we have a man who in his youth came, by God's grace, to accept the Christian faith wholeheartedly, but incompletely, even in some matters erroneously, and was then led on, in unique and providential circumstances, to recover it in a surprisingly balanced, full and pure form. We too wish to hold our faith in as balanced, full and pure a form as possible, both for our own sakes, and so that others may be drawn to it and it may be effective.

The first thing, then, to be done, is to sketch out

Newman's history, precisely in order to show how he recovered Christian truth in its fullness, and how justified we are in taking him as our guide now in the last quarter of the twentieth century.

There is another reason why the study of Newman's life is of such value. The first of his published sermons has for its title "Holiness necessary for future blessedness", and we see him during his long life pursuing the Christian ideal of holiness with a striking singleness of purpose. This was an essential element in his recovery of the Christian revelation. The truth is not reached by mere intellectual ability or learned study. It must be sought by the whole man, his faculties purified by obedience to the light of his moral conscience. The apostle St Paul speaks of those who are blind to the Gospel, and he speaks of them not as the uneducated and dull of understanding, but as the wise men, the scribes, the debaters of this age. Our Lord says the same, when he thanks his Father for hiding these things from the wise and prudent, and revealing them to little ones.

Moral dispositions and a moral stuggle are necessary if we are to attain to and possess the Gospel truth in its purity. It is not a passive reception. Newman's history is important not only for the prolonged intellectual striving towards the truth, but also for the moral struggle, the effort after holiness which accompanied it. To one of his sermons he gave the title "Truth hidden when not sought after" and he showed how the truth must be sought by the heart as well as by the head.

> It should not surprise us when men of acute and powerful understandings more or less reject the Gospel, for this reason, that the Christian revelation addresses itself to our hearts, to our love of truth and goodness, our fear of sinning, and our desire to gain God's favour; and quickness, sagacity, depth of thought, strength of mind, power of comprehension, perception of the beautiful,

> power of language, and the like, though they are excellent gifts, are clearly quite of a different kind from these spiritual excellencies—a man may have the one without having the other. *This*, then, is the plain reason why able, or again why learned men are so often defective Christians, because there is no necessary connexion between faith and ability; because faith is one thing and ability is another; because abilitv of mind is a *gift*, and faith is a *grace*.

And later in the same sermon:

> Seek truth in the way of *obedience*; try to act up to your conscience, and let your opinions be the result, not of mere chance reasoning or fancy, but of an improved heart. This way, I say, carries with it an evidence to ourselves of its being the right way, if any way be right; and that there is a right and a wrong way conscience also tells us. God surely will listen to none but those who strive to obey him.

Let us see, then, Newman beginning to practise what he was later to preach. Let us begin with the lesson of Newman's life.

John Henry Newman was born in 1801 in London, the son of a private banker, who was soon able to afford a second house, a fine Georgian one, still standing outside London, by the Thames at Ham. Newman's mother was a Fourdrinier, of French Huguenot descent. She was a good moderate Bible-reading Anglican, her husband somewhat more liberal in his religious opinions. John was the eldest of six children, three boys and three girls, and his first fifteen years were spent amid the affection of a happy and united family. The parents encouraged literature, music and amateur theatricals at home, and in the civilised boarding school at Ealing to which he was sent at the age of eight, the foundations of Newman's scholarship were laid.

Neither his home nor his school had been affected by the Evangelical revival, and religion consisted in the frequent reading of the Bible, rather than in rites or creeds. This English religion of the Bible Newman would later describe in *A Grammar of Assent*: "It consisted mainly in having the Bible read in Church, in the family and in private." It gave English people religious thoughts, a high moral standard and a sense of God's individual Providence. It was "not a religion of persons and things, of acts of faith and of direct devotion; but of sacred scenes and pious sentiments."[1] Thus although he had been taught his Anglican catechism, Newman could say that he had, as a boy, "no formed religious convictions".[2] He knew his Bible through and through, which was read to him by his mother and grandmother, before he was able to read it himself.

By the time he was fifteen, Newman had risen to the top of his school, and emerged as a leader among the boys. By this time, too, he had begun to read atheistical books and was toying with ideas of unbelief and of his own self-sufficiency. In the *Apologia* he tells us: "I recollect copying out some French verses, perhaps Voltaire's, against the immortality of the soul, and saying to myself something like 'How dreadful but how plausible'."[3] In a private note-book of 1823 he wrote: "I recollect (in 1815 I believe) thinking I should like to be virtuous, but not religious. There was something in the latter idea I did not like. Nor did I see the *meaning* of loving God."[4] Newman's was not yet a "religion of persons"— of personal friendship between himself and his Maker.

Now, however, came the turning point of his life, his first conversion, which he described in various of his writings. In the *Apologia* he wrote: "When I was fifteen (in the autumn of 1816) a great change of thought took place in me. I fell under the influence of a definite creed, and received into my intellect impressions of dogma, which through God's mercy, have never been effaced or obscured."[5]

Earlier in that same year the prosperity of the Newman family came to an end, in the depression after the Napoleonic Wars. The family had to move from London, and Newman himself was left at school for the last five months of the year, until the move was completed.

During that period he came under the influence of a young master at the school, Walter Mayers, a clergyman, who had recently undergone an evangelical conversion. Mayers lent him religious books, mostly Calvinistic ones, and by the end of 1816, Newman himself had experienced an evangelical conversion. This conversion, which took five months, was neither violent nor sudden, and by the end of it Newman had come to accept wholeheartedly the revealed religion of Christianity in the purest form available to him. From Mayers and from the books he lent, Newman learned the main dogmas of Christianity, and above all the fundamental one, faith in the Holy Trinity. The teaching on Father, Son and Holy Spirit, on the Incarnation and the Redemption had become a reality, as is shown by the prayers he now composed for his private use, and he tried to live the doctrine of the presence and indwelling of the Holy Spirit.[6] He gave full assent to the belief in eternal happiness, as well as in "eternal punishment as delivered by our Lord himself", and to what he calls the "Catholic doctrine of the warfare between the city of God and the powers of darkness". The Calvinist doctrine of predestination to eternal death Newman never accepted.[7] The great dogmas of the faith, so far from being in opposition to spiritual religion, were for him its very foundation. The unseen world had become real.

Newman now became an evangelical, and he accepted his new-found faith not only with his mind but also with his heart. Yet he called it a change of thought, to emphasise its intellectual character, and he already saw that there was a rational justification for his new certitudes. He was struck by their reflex character, "I know that I know", and by their consistency, the hall-mark of truth. With intellectual conviction went the whole-hearted striving for holiness. He began to "rest in the thought of two and two only absolute and luminously self-evident beings, myself and my Creator."[8] The visible world, so beautiful, was a veil for a more real world unseen. This was not incipient idealism, but a deep *Christian* way of thinking.

Nor did it make Newman neglect the world in which he lived. He made his own two evangelical mottoes, "life is for action" and "holiness before peace". For a parallel with Newman's first conversion, one might imagine a gifted unthinking boy for whom a retreat at school or the reading of some religious classic marked the beginning of a spiritual life, except that Newman speaks much more strongly. He was "made a Christian", he began a new life. It was the turning point which gave the rest of his life its unity. His unfolding mind was captured by the Christian revelation, and his heart by the Christian ideal of holiness.

Newman went up to Trinity College, Oxford, as an evangelical, and tried to live in God's presence. This interfered neither with hard work nor with the gathering round him of friends, as they were to gather, so numerous and of such distinction, right to the end of his life. In 1822 he was elected a Fellow of Oriel, then at the height of its fame, and was raised "from obscurity and need to competency and reputation".[9] He helped his brother at Oxford, and later his mother and sisters, and in the new liberal atmosphere he began to shed his peculiarly evangelical beliefs.

In June 1824 he received Ordination in the Church of England, regarding it as in no way a sacrament, but as the dedication of his life. He wrote a sentence which gives the key to all his subsequent history, "I have the responsibility of souls on me to the day of my death."[10] For two years he was in charge of the poor working class parish of St Clement in Oxford, where he visited everyone most diligently. He then became a tutor at Oriel, but only after assuring himself that this too was a pastoral office.

It was now ten years since he had accepted the Christian dogmas, and he was coming to see that these included belief in the Church as a divinely appointed visible body distinct from the state, and that in it was preserved and handed on the revelation. It was entered by the sacrament of baptism independently of any conversion experience. A little later Newman learned from the High Church Fellow of Oriel, Richard Hurrell Froude, the full doctrine of the sacraments, belief in the real presence, and devotion to the Mother of God.

Wishing to complete his hold on the revealed truths, Newman turned to the early Christian fathers, whom he had long admired. They were the true exponents of the doctrines of Christianity, and the basis of the High Church party in Anglicanism. From the year 1828 Newman began to read the Fathers systematically.[11] He went back to the sources, he engaged in that *resourcement*, which was to be such a feature of Catholicism in the middle of the twentieth century. Within four years, by the time the Oxford Movement began, we may say that he had recovered the Christian faith almost in its entirety. He did not, of course, accept the papacy, nor transubstantiation, or praying to saints. He did not, as yet, distinguish between mortal and venial sin, nor was he clear as to how post-baptismal sin was remitted, although these two points were gradually clarified.

In the same year 1828, Newman was appointed vicar of the university church of St Mary's, which had a parish attached to it. He was not, however, preacher to the university. He preached "parochial sermons" which were more and more appreciated by the younger graduates and undergraduates. Through them, and especially as they began to be published in book form, he came to exercise an extraordinary influence over educated people in England. There have been many descriptions of these sermons and their influence. The Anglican Dean Church wrote:

> A passionate and sustained earnestness after a high moral rule, seriously realised in conduct, is the dominant character of these sermons. They showed the strong reaction... against the poverty, softness, restlessness, worldliness, the blunted and impaired sense of truth, which reigned with little check in the recognised fashions of professing Christianity; the want of depth both of thought and feeling; the strange blindness to the real sternness, nay the austerity of the New Testament.[12]

Dean Church also tells us: "The most practical of sermons, the most real in their way of dealing with life and conduct, they are also intensely dogmatic."[13] That is the point which must above all be emphasised–the Christian faith was brought out in its fullness. Besides the sermons, Newman now published his first book, *The Arians of the Fourth Century*. It dealt with one of the great problems of revealed, dogmatic religion, the need to define and elaborate the truths given in Christ and enshrined in holy Scripture. This was a regrettable necessity–if truth was to be defended and handed on. It contains one of the finest expositions of the doctrine of the Holy Trinity.

This, then, is the first secret of Newman's influence, his submission to revealed religion. The more this is presented in its true proportions, the more it attracts and is effective. Even in the Catholic Church, which has the divine guarantee, it can, as we now readily admit, get surprisingly out of focus at different times and in different places. Newman did his best to provide a complete and balanced doctrine to sustain his hearers, derived from holy Scripture and the Fathers of the Church. His teaching was welcomed by many in the Church of England, where it inspired a great movement of renewal. It has also been received with ever increasing appreciation by the Catholic Church. The late Abbot Vonier used to sigh for a classical theology, where every truth of revelation would be stated in its proper proportion and balance, and not, as is so often the case, distorted, or exaggerated, or obscured by reaction against heresy or by popular devotion.[14]

Needless to say, it is impossible for anyone to work out the doctrines of Christianity, from the sources, completely *in vacuo*. All the same, Newman at Oxford was in a strikingly privileged position. Unlike the Roman theologians, he was brought up under the influence of no dominant philosophy or tradition of theology. If he made use of the seventeenth century Anglican divines, it was, as he confessed, rather to protect and defend what he had elaborated independently from holy Scripture and the fathers. If he reacted against heresy, it was against the general heresy which rejected revealed religion. And so it comes about that in Newman's Anglican writings we find a classical, a truly catholic Catholicism. He was devoted to the Greek fathers, and, as we shall see, there are to be found in his teaching many of the insights of the East, which the West is recovering.[15]

The next secret of Newman's influence is to realise that he was not a scholastic theologian or a university lecturer in theology working his subject out scientifically and in the abstract. He was a preacher and a pastor who wished men to build their lives on the God-given dogmatic foundations. Nor was he writing like an ascetic in his cell for the benefit of monks and nuns. The audience he had pastorally in view was that of lay people in the world, many of them far from committed to the faith they were supposed to hold. Their level of culture was high, but Newman did not condescend to them. He put before them the Christian ideal in its fullness. He had full sympathy with the problems of lay people, but he would not lower the demands that holiness required. He has been described as saying: "If you have a religion like Christianity, think of it and have it worthily." He was, then, a pastor, preaching to lay people, and yet among the places where he is most appreciated today are the monasteries of contemplative monks and nuns.

The result of Newman's work was that now many people in England began to lead spiritual, self-denying lives. The Oxford Movement was a doctrinal and spiritual revival. He and his friends began to publish the short "Tracts for the Times" which gave the Movement its name. At first they insisted on the doctrine of the Church as a divine institution, which derived its powers from the apostles. "We were upholding", said Newman later, "that primitive Christianity which was delivered for all time by the early teachers of the Church. . . that ancient religion had well nigh faded out of the land. . . and it must be restored."[16] Since example is more effective than exhortation, he brought out *The Church of the Fathers*, short articles in which he illustrated by means of biographical sketches, the atmosphere, the sentiments and the ideals of the early Church.

It was, however, his sermons, in which "he spoke like one who saw", which had most influence. According to one of many testimonies, they "came down like a new revelation. He had the wondrous, the supernatural power of raising the mind to God, and of rooting deeply in us the personal conviction of God, and a sense of his presence".[17]

Newman led the Movement for the next decade, and when he died the Anglican Dean Church described him as "the founder of the Church of England as we see it. What the Church of England would have become without the Tractarian Movement we can faintly guess. . . All that was best in Tractarianism came from him—its reality, its depth, its low estimate of externals, its keen sense of the importance of religion to the individual soul".[18]

It should be emphasised that in all this Newman was not trying to be original. The last thing he wanted was to be thought "a creative mind" or to be inventing some new theory. His whole aim was to discover and submit to the true tradition, the revelation that had been handed down. Hence his study of the fathers. He had no particular doctrine of his own. He was starting nothing new.

Furthermore, although he may certainly be described as a prophet, he was also very much a man, and not only a man but a humanist. Besides studying the Latin and Greek classics like all his contemporaries, he was a mathematician, and accomplished musician, and the bursar and even the wine-taster of his college. When he was asked what he thought of Wellington's Despatches, which had just been published, he replied: "Think, why they make one burn to be a soldier." He was intensely interested in the persons and the world around him, and all that related to them. From his schooldays until ripe old age he was full of activity and surrounded by friends. What struck all who knew him was the absence of pomposity, that naturalness which is the consequence of sincerity with oneself.

But with it all, he was detached. In later life he was able to write in a private note-book, addressing his Maker, "When I was young I thought with all my heart that I gave up the world for thee. As far as will, purpose, and intention go, I think I did. I mean I deliberately put the world aside."[19] As the spiritual leader of the English elite at Oxford, the highest prizes might have been his, if he had been ready to stoop a little. The old President of Magdalen College, Dr Routh, remarked early on, that, different from his contemporaries, "Mr Newman is not trying to get on in life". Newman revealed himself when he made the pagan heroine in his novel *Callista* remark "that there was a higher beauty than that which the order and harmony of the natural world revealed, and a deeper peace and calm than that which the exercise, whether of the intellect or the purest human affection, can supply". Christians "were detached from the world, not because they had not the possession, nor the natural love of its gifts, but because they possessed a higher blessing already, which they loved above everything else."[20]

Newman's detachment was now to be put to the test. In the summer of 1839 when continuing his patristic studies, he was struck by the resemblance of Protestants and Anglicans respectively to the extreme and moderate heretics who rejected the Council of Chalcedon. Shortly afterwards he was even more struck by an article by the future Cardinal Wiseman, which described St Augustine's way of deciding the controversy with the Donatists,[21] his appeal to the general consent of Christians. *Securus judicat orbis terrarum*, the judgment of the whole world cannot be mistaken. There was a simpler way of deciding ecclesiastical questions than the appeal to the early centuries. That "in which the whole Church rests and acquiesces, is an infallible prescription and a final sentence against such portions of it as protest and secede."[22]

It was obvious that the Anglican Church was separated from the rest of Christendom. The counter charge that the Catholic Church had added unjustifiably to the original revelation, was not so clear. The revival by the Tractarians of the forgotten doctrines about the Church as a body deriving its authority from the apostles was intended to provide a basis against the encroachments of the state, but it at once drew attention to the isolated position of the Church of England.

Newman's followers began to feel that there was so much Protestantism in that Church as to invalidate its claim to be a "branch" Church.[23] In 1841 he wrote the last of the Tracts, *No. 90*, to meet this difficulty and to save them from becoming Catholics. Others had seen the ghost. To show the catholicity of his Church he did his best to reconcile Anglican and Catholic doctrine. It was an exercise in ecumenism. Catholics had been guilty of exaggerations in their popular practice, Anglicans were too imbued with Protestantism. The Church of England as a whole rejected the Tract, and thus its claim to be "Catholic". On the other hand the whole Christian world rejected the "branch theory" and did not regard the Church of England as part of the Catholic Church. Newman tried hard to treat his doubts as illusions, but two years later he was writing to Keble: "I am far *more* certain that England is in schism, than that the Roman additions to the primitive creed may not be developments, arising out of a keen and vivid realisation of the depositum."[24] the New Testament revelation.

Newman was thus led to examine more deeply the question of how far revealed religion could develop.

In his first book he had noticed how from the earliest times Christians, in order to defend or transmit their faith, had been obliged to elaborate and define beyond the actual words of Scripture. The Christian revelation, however, was not a series of propositions, but historical events, with the incarnation at their centre. Now, in 1843, in the sermon on "The Theory of Developments in Religious Doctrine" he dealt with the subject *ex professo*. He insisted that the knowledge a Christian had of his faith was distinct from its explicit statement. "The absence or partial absence or incompleteness of dogmatic statements is no proof of the absence of impressions or implicit judgments in the mind of the Church. Even centuries might pass without formal expression of a truth, which had been all along the secret life of millions of faithful souls".[25] For the protection and understanding of their revelation Christians are led to make statements about the object of their adoration, and what is essentially an impression on the mind and imagination becomes a system and a creed. "Creeds and dogmas live in the one idea which they are designed to express, and which alone is substantive; and are necessary only because the human mind cannot reflect upon that idea except piecemeal, cannot use it in its oneness and entirety."[26]

Newman was describing what was to be one of the chief insights of the Second Vatican Council, that the truth of revelation is not a mere series of propositions, but "shines forth for us in Christ who is at once the mediator and the fullness of revelation".[27] Thus we can believe what we can't explain. All Christians have a reason, not all can give a reason.

The sermon also shows Newman's prophetic grasp of Christian truth, "the vision of an Object", the self-disclosure of God, which, far from being enclosed in the propositions necessary to state it, would not be exhausted by many more. Hence, the Anglican Newman points out, to want to have every doctrine in so many words in Scripture is to be the slave of the letter.

The theory of development provided an answer to the difficulty which held Newman back from the Roman Church, namely that it had tampered with and added to the revelation. A further conclusion followed from this. If Christianity was a universal religion, adapted to every age and place, it must develop. If so it was antecedently most probable that there must be a living authority, able to distinguish between true and false developments, able to protect the life-giving revelation. This could only be the Church, which Scripture called the "Pillar and ground of truth", and Newman had long taught that it was indefectible. "Surely, either an objective religion has not been given, or it has been provided with the means of impressing its objectiveness on the world."[28]

As an Anglican he had appealed to antiquity–the faith of the ancient Church before it split into branches, was the source of truth: "My bulwark was the fathers."[29] Although he now recognised that there must be a living present authority, his principle still held: that Church was the Church of Christ which was historically the successor of the Church of the fathers. Christ had left behind a divine society. That society, which existed in ancient times, could not fail. It must exist now, and—final step—the Roman Church was identical with the Church of the fathers, which it was the gravest of duties to join.

This meant abandoning all he loved best in the world, breaking with his friends and with his own family, and social ostracism. Becoming a Catholic in England in the mid-nineteenth century had far graver social consequences than becoming a Communist in the mid-twentieth. Pusey continued to write, but the correspondence with Keble and Church petered out, and they and so many others kept aloof for twenty years.

Worst of all was the knowledge that his teaching had brought so many to the practice of a real Christian life, and that they would now be thrown into confusion, and would go back, perhaps even fall in to scepticism and unbelief. The Catholic Church itself, as it existed in the concrete in England, not to say elsewhere, appeared very unattractive, and would continue to do so. Newman knew this perfectly well, but he was driven on by his state of unbroken certainty, which he had tried to treat as an illusion. He wrote to Keble in November 1844: "I am setting my face absolutely towards the wilderness",[30] and in December: "No one can have a more unfavourable view that I of the present state of the Roman Catholics—so much so, that any who join them would be like the Cistercians at Fountains [Abbey], living under trees till their house was built. If I must account for it, I should say that want of unity has injured both them and us."[31]

On 9 October 1845 Newman was received into the

Catholic Church by Blessed Dominic Barberi, a most unlikely human agent, but a saint, and for him the step was a simple corollary of his first conversion at sixteen, when he had accepted wholeheartedly the Christian revelation. From that time and more specifically from his Anglican ordination in 1824, he had one single purpose, which gave his life its unity, a pastor's devotion to the revealed religion of Christianity. Thus, although he now began a new life in a different world, he changed very little. In the *Apologia* he wrote: "I was not conscious to myself on my conversion, of any change, intellectual or moral, wrought in my mind. I was not conscious of firmer faith in the fundamental truths of revelation, or of more self-command; I had not more fervour; but it was like coming into port after a rough sea".[32]

His new beliefs were peripheral. He did not alter his doctrine of the Church, but acknowledged the Catholic Church of his day to be that of St Ambrose and St Athanasius. On its authority he accepted the papacy. He had long believed in the real presence, he now added to it the doctrine of transubstantiation. He accepted the doctrine of purgatory, indulgences and the invocation of saints. Belief in their intercession had always been an Anglican tenet. In the same way as regards prayer and devotion: although he added Catholic practices such as the rosary and visits to the Blessed Sacrament, he still kept to the formulas of his youth. The early prayers he had composed or adapted after his first conversion were copied out again in the booklets he read, to the end of his life, during his thanksgiving after Mass. The very intentions, particularised, of his prayers, he continued to use almost unchanged. As Dom Placid Murray has remarked: "Here, if anywhere, we can find that intimate continuity and identity which make the Vicar of St Mary's, the Father of the Oratory, and the Cardinal of the Roman Church into one and the same man".[33]

Nevertheless, "we must throw ourselves into the

system",[34] he told his friends and disciples, for at this period several hundred university and educated men, some of the leading intellectuals of the day, with their wives and families, became Catholics. He had to settle his own vocation and that of the small group who wished to throw in their lot with him. He considered joining various religious orders, but realised that his previous life was intended to be the means of future usefulness. To a friend he wrote: "Having lived so long in Oxford, my name and person are known to a very great many people I do not know—so are my books—and I may have begun a work I am now to finish. Now the question is whether as a regular I do not at once cut off all this, as becoming a sort of instrument of others, and so clean beginning life again. As a Jesuit, for example, no one would know that I was speaking my own words: or was a *continuation*, as it were of my former self".[35] This was one of the advantages of the Oratory of St Philip, which was not a religious order, but a group of ordinary priests living together. There too his friends could join him, but especially he was attracted by St Philip, led by the Holy Spirit, with his naturalness and hatred of all pretence, so modern and yet so scriptural. Oratories could be founded in the new large towns, which Newman saw as the centres of the future.

Newman's Catholic life was spent in trying to remedy the deficiencies and check the tendencies which made it so difficult for people to see in the Church, as he had, "the one fold of the Redeemer".[36] The great Christian privileges and the divine indwelling, which he had preached at Oxford, were insufficiently appreciated. The laity were in need of education and their position in the Church was sadly underestimated, as indeed was that of bishops, as against the ever more centralised papacy.

Another crying need was the intellectual defence of revealed religion, against the rising tide of unbelief.

Newman set up the first English Oratory at Birmingham in 1848, and it formed the framework for the rest of his life. There he worked among the poor for two years, until appointed by the Pope and the Irish bishops the first Rector of a Catholic University in Dublin for the English-speaking world.

Education was one of the many Catholic deficiencies, and for seven years Newman spent the best part of his time in Ireland on a work intended primarily to benefit the laity. With careful attention to practical detail he founded the university, and if the bishops had given him a free hand it would have been a great success. It was to subserve the cause of religion, but Newman insisted in his lectures on *The Idea of a University* that it had its own sufficient end, the enlargement of mind. He endeared himself to the Irish, and reflected long afterwards: "It was not Ireland that was unkind to me. The same thing would have happened in England or France. It was the clergy, moved as they are in automaton fashion by the camarilla at Rome."[37] It was no longer necessary to defend the authority of hierarchy and clergy. What needed emphasising was that the Church was the communion of all its members. So Newman continued to work for the laity.

On 2 May 1857 he started a small boarding school to provide as good an education for their sons as that open to Protestants, and in 1859 he undertook the editorship of the *Rambler*, the only high-class Catholic review, threatened with censure by the bishops. After the second number he was delated to Rome for defending the right of the laity to be consulted even in matters of faith. The Church for him was all who had been baptised and received the Spirit, but under the dominant clericalism they had a passive role. He remarked that the Church would look foolish without them. He obediently gave up the *Rambler* because "if you do the right thing at the wrong time, you become a heretic".[38]

In 1864 he was challenged to defend his integrity, and the resulting *Apologia* won for him a public position in England, which he had not had since 1845. "Life is for action,"[39] and he at once used his new power in attempts to make provision for the university education of Catholics by founding a house of the Oratory at Oxford. This was at the request of the bishop responsible, but Archbishop Manning ensured that Catholics were forbidden to attend universities.

For Newman, whether in going to Oxford or his other labours, conversions were not the first thing, but raising the level of Catholics. The Church must be prepared for converts, he said, as well as converts for the Church. He wished to see Christians reach a common mind, and republished his Anglican writings with this in view. That was how the unity would be attained, for which he had prayed ever since the days of his first conversion. He acknowledged all that was valuable in the Anglican communion, and tried to temper Catholic extremism and other obstacles to unity on his own side. When in 1866 Pusey attacked exaggerated Catholic devotion to the blessed Virgin, Newman defended the true kind, basing himself on the fathers, "who made me a Catholic",[40] but rejected the exaggerations which did such harm. In a revealed religion devotion must derive from dogma.

At this time, too, Newman was writing his last major work, *G. A.* It dealt with a question that had occupied him all his life: the justification people have for being certain of things they have not been able to prove. He had defended the right of ordinary man to his certitudes in *U. S.*, and now he perfected it in his old age. It was a fact that men were certain of many things they could not absolutely prove. This did not mean that the act of faith or other certainties were not based on reason, but that the full basis of them could not be put into words. "All men reason, but not all men can give a reason."[41]

Newman thus rejected the view of much traditional Catholic apologetics that there was a completely satisfactory way of expressing arguments for faith in logical form. He appealed to the facts. Men were certain, but their certainty was personal, depending on their character or on reasons they had not brought home to themselves. The moral sense enabled men to judge rightly in matters of religious duty, just as experience sharpened their powers in other spheres. Thus the shepherd can foretell the weather, and the general interpret information, apparently without reasoning. When our minds are working naturally they are guided to certainty by antecedent considerations and by numberless cumulative indications, by reasons personal to each individual. If, as has sometimes been thought, the reasons for faith must be put into strict logical form, then only learned theologians could have reasonable certainties. Newman appeals to the facts to defend the reasonableness of the faith of ordinary people. But all this will be developed later.

In 1870 came the definition of papal infallibility. Newman, who as an Anglican held that the Church was indefectible, accepted the doctrine on becoming a Catholic, but thought a definition unnecessary and inexpedient. A violent campaign seemed to turn the Pope into an oracle independent of the Church, and Newman spent much of his time re-assuring ordinary Catholics. The prerogative involved only a negative protection, and the definitions of a future council would, he thought, limit it still further. Above all he appealed to *securus judicat orbis terrarum,* "the judgment of the whole Church has no chance of being wrong".[42] While dogmas were sacred as the essential basis of spiritual religion, outside them Newman insisted throughout his life as a Catholic on the value and expedience of free discussion in the Church. Theologians could not work like Persian soldiers, "under the lash". He advocated "a wise and gentle minimism". Almost his last publication, on the inspiration of Scripture, was written, not to settle matters but to keep them open.

Newman's elevation to the cardinalate in 1879 by Leo XIII vindicated him against all those who had labelled him as unsound, a Gallican, or "only half a Catholic", and set the approval of the Church on his labours for revealed religion. Long before that he held an eminent though private position in England, looked up to and consulted on religious problems by people of the most diverse beliefs. An Anglican clergyman wrote to him in 1879: "I wonder if any man, at least in our time, was ever so loved by England–by all religiously-minded England. And even the enemies of faith are softened by their feeling for you. And I wonder whether this extraordinary and unparalleled love might not be–was not meant to be–utilised, as one means to draw into one fold all Englishmen who believe. I can conceive no more powerful nor truer *eirenicon*".[43]

Newman's two lives, Anglican and Catholic, seemed to move towards unity, or rather that first conversion in 1816 gave all his life its unity. All else flowed from it. He himself bore his witness, writing shortly before he died, "testifying my simple love and adhesion to the Catholic Roman Church. . . and did I wish to give a reason for this full and absolute devotion, what should, what can I say but that those great and burning truths which I learned when a boy from evangelical teaching, I have found impressed upon my heart with fresh and ever increasing force by the Holy Roman Church".[44]

The first lesson of Newman's life is that of a great effort to recover the full Christian truth and to present it in all its primitive attractiveness. Newman also tried to remedy some of the deficiencies in the Catholic Church of his day. In a letter of 1882 when he was a cardinal, which was translated into Italian and read to Leo XIII,

Newman spoke of what he called "nihilism in the Catholic body, and its rulers. They forbid but they do not direct or create".[45] The deficiencies remained, some even became worse after his death. He had tried to do a work and been thwarted, but he hoped and half realised that his labours and trials and patient obedience would bear fruit in the future.

Unexpectedly "a man was sent from God whose name was John", and at the Second Vatican Council the tides of clericalism, over-centralisation, creeping infallibility, narrow unhistorical theology and exaggerated mariology were thrown back, while the things Newman fought for were brought forward—freedom, the supremacy of conscience, the Church as a communion, a return to Scripture and the fathers, the rightful place of the laity, work for unity, and all the efforts to meet the needs of the age, and for the Church to take its place in the modern world. Any disarray or confusion there may now be in the Church is the measure of how necessary this renewal was, and may be seen as the inevitable result of the policy of nihilism.

Many today seem to find in Newman an inspiration for the work of renewal. He combines utter firmness of faith with great openness. He sought the truth, he suffered for it, and the serenity which underlies all his writing surely bears witness to the fact that he had found it. The truth is hidden when not sought after, and Newman teaches us that it is to be sought not only with the mind but also with the heart and by the way of obedience, by means of that holiness without which no man will see God.

2 Personal influence

If belief in revealed religion was crumbling in Newman's day it has crumbled still more since. If a sense of the unseen world needed revivifying then, it needs it even more today. Surely what the Catholic Church is crying out for is an Oxford Movement, a reinvigoration of dogmatic religion with its consequences in spiritual revival. Her deficiences need to be made good so that she may appear in her primitive attractiveness in a world where so many have lost their bearings and are hungering for religion. We share Newman's pastoral and apostolic aims. How can he help us?

Newman always dated the beginning of the Oxford Movement from Keble's sermon in July 1833 on national apostasy, when he denounced the interference of the State in the religious affairs of the Church, but it is not clear that the sermon made much stir. It was preached during the vacation, Pusey did not cut the pages of his copy of it. In it Keble preached resignation to the evils of the day. It is true that very soon afterwards the *Tracts for the Times* began, but Newman's sermons were having their effect and leading people to lead religious lives long before.

It has in fact been maintained that the Oxford Movement was really launched in another sermon preached eighteen months earlier, in January 1832, Newman's, entitled "Personal influence the means of propagating the Truth".[1]

He examined the question of how revealed religion was to be handed on. How were principles perpetuated which were distasteful even to the majority of those who professed to receive them. For "the natural man does not receive the gifts of the Spirit of God, for they are folly to him" (*1 Cor 2:14*). It was a case not merely of passing on a number of propositions by means of argument but of ensuring profound belief, of changing hearts. The proud and sensual were irritated into opposition by the Christian doctrines, the philosophic considered them strange and chemerical. "For in truth," says Newman, "what was the task of an apostle, but to raise the dead?"[2] Error had so many advantages in the struggle with truth. Reason with its smoothly formulated arguments seemed to support it, while Faith dealt with matters too sacred and too mysterious easily to be put into words at all. How then was the Truth upheld?

"I answer, that it has been upheld in the world not as a system, not by books, not by argument, not by temporal power, but by the personal influence of such men as [are] at once the teachers and patterns of it."[3]

And Newman explains: "Men persuade themselves with little difficulty to scoff at principles, to ridicule books, to make sport of the names of good men; but they cannot bear their presence: it is holiness embodied in personal form, which . . . they cannot steadily confront and bear down."[4]

Even in an irreligious age people are on the look-out for men of God, and when they see rare perfection, they watch it with a mixture of curiosity and awe. It is a matter of acts, not words. "One little deed, done against natural inclination for God's sake, though in itself of a conceding or passive character, to brook an insult, to face a danger, or to resign an advantage, has in it a power outbalancing all the dust and chaff of mere profession."[5]

Furthermore, although unbelief seems to triumph, and although men as a body appear to be self-sufficient, yet to each one individually there comes adversity or affliction. Then they learn how "Glory, science, knowledge, never healed a wounded heart or changed a sinful one", they realise their inadequacy, and are open to good influences. It is difficult to over-estimate the moral power which a single individual, trained to practise what he teaches, may acquire in his own circle in the course of years. The attraction exerted by unconscious holiness is irresistible, and gradually men become aware of Christ's presence among them.

In a famous passage Newman continues his argument:

"But, after all, say they are few, such high Christians; and what follows? They are enough to carry on God's noiseless work. The apostles were such men; others might be named, in their several generations, as successors to their holiness. These communicate their light to a number of lesser luminaries, by whom in its turn, it is distributed through the world... A few highly endowed men will rescue the world for centuries to come."[6] And Newman went on to refer to St Athanasius, who, almost alone, had preserved and impressed upon the Church the true doctrine of our Lord's divinity.

That was the programme of the Oxford Movement, by unconscious personal holiness to preserve and spread the full Christian truth. Newman himself is the primary example of this, and we have already seen the sources of the ascendancy he exercised, his sense of the unseen world and his integrity. Personal influence is the means of propagating the truth. Newman held to this all his life, as the choice he made of his motto as Cardinal shows, *Cor ad cor loquitur*.

He had explained the point of it long before, in his paper on University Preaching:

> He who has before his mental eye the Four Last Things will have the true earnestness, the horror or the rapture, of one who witnesses a conflagrat-ion, or discerns some rich and sublime prospect of natural scenery. His countenance, his manner, his voice, speak for him, in proportion as his view has

> been vivid and minute. . . As the case would be with one who has actually seen what he relates, the herald of tidings of the invisible world also will be, from the nature of the case, whether vehement or calm, sad or exulting, always simple, grave, emphatic, and peremptory; and all this, not because he has proposed to himself to be so, but because certain intellectual convictions involve certain external manifestations. St Francis de Sales is full and clear on this point. It is necessary, he says, (Newman quotes in Latin), "estre bien espris de la doctrine qu'on enseigne et de ce qu'on persuade. Le souverain artifice c'est de n'avoir point de'artifice. Il faut que nos paroles soyent enflammees, non pas par des cris et actions desmesurees, mais par l'affection interieure; il faut qu'elles sortent du coeur plus que de la bouche. On a beau dire, mais le coeur parle au coeur, et la langue ne parle qu'aux oreilles." *Cor cordi loquitur.*[7]

"Intellectual convictions involve external manifestations." This is the underlying assumption behind the principle that personal influence is the means of propagating the truth. It leads on to another point which Newman held to be of the greatest importance, and which he was continually emphasising. If men are to lead lives of self-sacrificing holiness, if they are to instil their ideals into others, they must have absolute conviction, be utterly certain of their own faith.

Here Newman found even Keble unsatisfactory. Keble was ready to argue it was highly probable that the Christian religion was true, and this probability was somehow converted into certainty by faith and love. "It is often taught," Newman says in the *Apologia*, "that probability is the guide of life. The danger of this doctrine in the case of many minds is its tendency to destroy in them absolute certainty, leaving them to consider every opinion as doubtful, and resolving truth into an opinion, which it is safe indeed to obey or to profess, but not possible to embrace with full internal assent. If this were to be allowed, then the celebrated saying, 'God, if there be a God, save my soul, if I have a soul!' would be the highest measure of devotion—but who can really pray to a Being about whose existence he is seriously in doubt!"[8]

In *A Grammar of Assent* Newman wrote:

> Without certitude in religious faith there may be much decency of profession and of observance, but there can be no habit of prayer, no directness of devotion, no intercourse with the unseen, no generosity of self-sacrifice. Certainty, then, is essential to the Christian; and if he is to presevere to the end, his certitude must include in it a principle of persistence.

And again:

> If religion is to be devotion, and not a mere matter of sentiment, if it is to be made the ruling principle of our lives, if our actions one by one, and our daily conduct, are to be consistently directed towards an Invisible Being, we need something higher than a mere balance of arguments to fix and control our minds. Sacrifice of wealth, name, or position, faith and hope, self-conquest, communion with the spiritual world, presuppose a real hold and habitual intuition of the objects of Revelation, which is certitude under another name.[9]
>
> Doubt and devotion are incompatible with each other; every doubt, be it greater or less, stronger or weaker, involuntary as well as voluntary, acts upon devotion so far forth, as water sprinkled, or dashed, or poured out upon a flame. Real and proper doubt kills faith, and devotion with it; and even involuntary or half deliberate doubt, though it does not actually kill faith, goes far to kill devotion; and religion without devotion is little

> better than a burden, and soon becomes superstition.[10]

All this amounts to and is an emphatic assertion of what we are told in the Epistle to the Hebrews: "Whoever would draw near to God must believe that he exists and that he rewards those who seek him."[11]

Newman was thus led in two of his works to defend the right of the ordinary man to his certitudes, in the *University Sermons* when he was at Oxford and in *A Grammar of Assent* in his old age. It was a fact that men were certain of many things they could not absolutely prove. This did not mean that the act of faith or other certainties were not based on reason, but that the full basis of them could not be put into words. "All men reason but not all men can give a reason."[12] And elsewhere: "It is hardly too much to say, that almost all reasons formally adduced in moral inquiries, are rather specimens and symbols of the real grounds, than those grounds themselves. They do but approximate to a representation of the general character of the proof which the writer wishes to convey to another's mind. They cannot, like mathematical proof, be passively followed with an attention confined to what is stated, and with admission of nothing but what is urged."[13]

Newman thus rejected the view of much traditional Catholic apologetics that there was a completely satisfactory way of expressing the arguments for faith in logical form. He appealed to the facts. Men were certain, but their certainty was personal, depending on their character or on reasons they had not brought home to themselves. The moral sense enables men to judge rightly in matters of religious duty, just as experience can sharpen their powers in other spheres. Thus the shepherd can foretell the weather and the general interpret information, apparently without reasoning. "Consider the preternatural sagacity with which a general knows what his friends and his enemies are about, and what will be the final result and where, of their combined movements, and then say whether, if he were required to argue the matter in word or on paper, all his most brilliant conjectures might not be refuted, and all his producible reasons exposed as illogical."[14]

Certitude is personal, but it is not made on weak or insufficient grounds. The believer who makes the act of faith has his reasons, and is satisfied that they are adequate, even though he may not be able to express them. When our minds are working naturally they are guided to certainty by antecedent considerations and by numberless cumulative indications, by reasons personal to each individual. If, as has so often been taught, the reasons for faith must be put into strict logical form, then only, at best, learned theologians could have reasonable certainties. Newman is defending the right of ordinary people to their certitudes, especially their religious certitudes. So far from being a fideist, he insists that the simplest of the faithful have reasonable grounds for their certitudes.

This is not the place to develop at greater length Newman's views on certainty, which have been reaffirmed by later thinkers and by psychological study. They confirm the great importance Newman attached to the need for certainty in matters of religion. Yet he was fully aware of the prevalence of doubt, and knew the difficulty of living a life of faith in an age of doubt. He was very sympathetic with inquirers and with those who wished to believe, telling them to make the most of the certainties they already had, and to be faithful to conscience and to grace.

To show how certainty was attained he appealed to the action of the moral conscience. Perhaps his most characteristic teaching was his appeal to conscience as the way to truth. It has been said that just as we have the Angelic Doctor and the Subtle Doctor, Newman is

Doctor Conscientiae. His views on this subject are so closely linked with his views on how personal certainty is reached and on how personal influence is made to bear, that they deserve to be developed at length.

He always insisted that the moral conscience was "the voice of God". He knew well enough how in modern times, long before psychoanalysis, great efforts were made to dismiss it as a mere work of man. He based his doctrine on the facts as he saw them:

"The child keenly understands that there is a difference between right and wrong; and when he has done what he believes to be wrong, he is conscious that he is offending One to whom he is amenable, whom he does not see, who sees him. His mind reaches forward with a strong presentiment to the thought of a moral governor, sovereign over him, mindful and just. It comes to him like an impulse of nature to entertain it." He noted that each man had within him a moral dictate, "an authoritative voice, bidding him to do certain things and avoid others". Its injunctions were not always clear in particular cases, not always consistent, but it praised, blamed and issued commands. In fact, although indivisible, its action was twofold; it was a dictate or sense of duty. It was also a judgment of the reason, that certain acts were good and certain others wicked, which persisted even where the obligation, the duty was rejected. A man had not power over it, or only with extreme difficulty, and he could never entirely destroy it.[15]

Thus the moral conscience from the nature of the case carries our mind to a Being outside ourselves, and far superior to us, with a peremptory claim on our obedience. Not only does it instruct us to a certain extent but it leads us to the idea of an unseen Teacher. It is not subjective merely nor even exclusively a moral faculty, but transcendent. The more men listen to and obey it, the clearer it becomes until it produces an intimate perception and sense of the one God. God is not reached by abstract external proofs but by a man's whole personality. As he purifies and strengthens this by faithfulness to his true self, he becomes apt, disposed, to accept and believe in the true God. Here are Newman's own words in the sermon "Dispositions for Faith":

> Whether a man has heard the name of the Saviour of the world or not. . . he has within his breast a certain commanding dictate, not a mere sentiment, nor a mere opinion, or impression, or view of things, but a law, an authoritative voice, bidding him do certain things and avoid others. I do not say that its particular injunctions are always clear, or that they are always consistent with each other; but what I am insisting on here is this, that it *commands*—that it praises, it blames, it promises, it threatens, it implies a future, and it witnesses of the unseen. It is more than a man's own self. The man himself has not power over it, or only with extreme difficulty; he did not make it, he cannot destroy it. . . This is Conscience; and from the nature of the case, its very existence carries on our minds to a Being exterior to ourselves; for else whence did it come? and to a Being superior to ourselves; else whence its strange troublesome peremptoriness? I say, without going on to the question *what* it says, and whether its particular dictates are always as clear and consistent as they might be, its very existence throws us out of ourselves, to go and seek for him in the height and depth, whose Voice it is.[16]

In the novel *Callista*, which contains some of Newman's finest teaching on the way to faith, the pagan heroine says: "I feel myself in his presence. He says to me 'Do this: don't do that.' You may tell me that this dictate is a mere law of my nature, as is to joy or to grieve. I cannot understand this. No, it is the echo of a person speaking to me. Nothing shall persuade me that it does not ultimately proceed from a person external to me. It carries with it its proof of its divine origin. My nature feels towards it as towards a person. When I obey it, I feel a satisfaction; when I disobey, a soreness—just like that which I feel in pleasing or offending some revered friend."[17]

We have already seen Newman showing how in ordinary matters knowledge depends on personality. The man of the world, thanks to a wide experience, can size up those he meets almost at a glance, and for him it is a very valuable asset. He could not put into words why he is prepared to trust this man and not that. His sharpened mind is working in its natural concrete manner. Similarly, in the sphere of religion, it is his moral disposition, his mind sharpened by obedience to conscience, which enables a man to realise the unseen and to have faith. It is not arguments that convince him, although these have their place and may enable him to justify his position to others. Moral dispositions are the road to the truth.

To quote Newman once more:

> This word within us not only instructs us up to a certain point, but necessarily raises our minds to the idea of a Teacher, an unseen Teacher: and in proportion as we listen to that word, and use it, not only do we learn more from it, not only do its dictates become clearer, and its lessons broader, and its principles more consistent, but its very tone is louder and more authoritative and constraining. And thus it is, that to those who use what they have, more is given; for, beginning with obedience, they go on to the intimate perception and belief of one God. His voice within them witnesses to him, and they believe his own witness about himself. They believe in his existence, not because others say it, not on the word of man merely, but with a personal apprehension of its truth.[18]

In order to receive distant transmissions a delicate, carefully prepared instrument is needed.

Obedience to conscience leads men further still. Often they cannot decide how much the "true inward guide commands, and how much comes from a mere earthly source. So that the gift of conscience raises a desire for what it does not itself fully supply. . . It creates in them a thirst, an impatience, for the knowledge of that unseen Lord and Governor, and Judge, who as yet speaks to them only secretly, who whispers in their hearts, who tells them something, but not nearly so much as they wish and as they need."[19]

Hence the conscientious man is led to look out for a revelation. It is the definition of a religious man who is not a Christian, that he is on the look-out. This, Newman explains, is why faith receives such praise in the Gospel, and incredulity such blame. Not only that, but the more a man obeys his conscience, the more he feels alarmed at himself for obeying it so imperfectly. He realises his need for clearer guidance and for more strength. Thus good moral dispositions lead on to faith, that is to an entire submission to God, and our great internal teacher of religion is our conscience. It is a personal guide, even though, since men do not live alone, external assistance may be necessary to help it into action.

Newman ends his sermon on "Dispositions for Faith" as follows:

> This is a day in which much stress is laid upon the *arguments* producible for believing religion, natural and revealed; and books are written to prove that we ought to believe and why. . . Now I have no intention whatever of denying the beauty and the cogency of the argument which these books contain; but I question much, whether in matter of fact they make or keep men Christians. I have no such doubt about the argu-

> ment which I have here been recommending to you. Be sure, my brethren, that the best argument, better than all the books in the world. . . an argument intelligible to those who cannot read as well as to those who can—an argument which is "within us", an argument intellectually conclusive, and practically persuasive, whether for proving the Being of a God, or for laying the ground for Christianity—is that which arises out of a careful attention to the teachings of our heart, and a comparison between the claims of conscience and the announcements of the Gospel.[20]

To avoid any misunderstanding there are two points that should be made clear in all this. First, that Newman takes for granted and assumes that God's hidden grace is at work in all men and leading them to faith. He is abstracting from grace, which is everywhere at work, and considering the outward phenomena. Second, the personal argument that leads men to faith is justified in reason, even though it may not be able to be stated in words by one who is convinced by it. It is the reason working naturally, not the reason working syllogistically, which tells a man he ought to believe.

Newman is quite clear that conviction is one thing and faith another. Faith is a gift of God, even though it follows upon an act of reason. In the sermon on "Faith and Doubt", he says:

> I may see that I ought to believe; and yet be unable to believe. . . conviction is not faith. Take the parallel case of obedience; many a man knows he ought to obey God, and does not and cannot—through his own fault, indeed—but still he cannot; for through grace only can he obey. Now, faith is not a mere conviction in reason, it is a firm assent, it is a clear certainty greater than any other certainty; and it is wrought in the mind by the grace of God, and by it alone. As then men may be convinced, and not act according to their

> conviction, so they may be convinced, and not believe according to their conviction. . . Their reason is convinced, and their doubts are moral ones, arising in their root from a fault of the will. In a word, the arguments for religion do not compel anyone to believe, just as the arguments for good conduct do not compel anyone to obey. Obedience is the consequence of willing to obey, and faith is the consequence of willing to believe.[21]

Newman describes both the certainty and the actual grounds of his faith. He says that the being of God

> is as certain to me as the certainty of my own existence, though when I try to put the grounds of that certainty into logical shape I find a difficulty in doing so in mood and figure to my satisfaction. . . I look out of myself into the world of men, and there I see a sight which fills me with unspeakable distress. The world seems simply to give the lie to that great truth, of which my whole being is so full. . . If I looked into a mirror, and did not see my face, I should have the sort of feeling which actually comes upon me, when I look into this busy living world, and see no reflection of its creator. . . Were it not for this voice, speaking so clearly in my conscience and my heart, I should be an atheist, or a pantheist, or a polytheist when I looked into the world. I am speaking for myself only; and I am far from denying the real force of the arguments in proof of a God, drawn from the general facts of human society and the course of history, but these do not warm or enlighten me.[22]

This was no new idea. In an Oxford University sermon Newman had said: "It is indeed a great question whether atheism is not as philosophically consistent with the phenomena of the physical world, taken by themselves, as the doctrine of a creating and governing power." When he republished this sermon as a Catholic,

Newman added a note: "'*Physical* phenomena, *taken by themselves*'; that is, apart from psychological phenomena, apart from moral considerations, apart from the moral principles by which they must be interpreted, and apart from the idea of God which wakes up in the mind under the stimulus of intellectual training."[23]

Perhaps his clearest statement is in the lecture on "Christianity and Physical Science" delivered in Dublin. He speaks of those attributes of God which are immediately connected with religious attitudes, his sanctity, omniscience, justice, mercy, faithfulness.

> What does physical theology, what does the argument from design, what do fine disquisitions about final causes, teach us, except very indirectly, faintly, enigmatically, of these transcendently important, these essential portions of the idea of religion? Religion is more than theology; it is something relative to us; and it includes our relation towards the Object of it. What does physical theology tell us of duty and conscience? of a particular providence? and, coming at length to Christianity, what does it teach us even of the four last things, death, judgment, heaven and hell, the mere elements of Christianity? It cannot tell us anything of Christianity at all.[24]

Later, in a letter of 1870, Newman wrote: "Something I must assume, and in assuming conscience I assume what is least to assume, and what most men will admit. Half the world knows nothing of the argument from design—and when you have got it, you do not prove by it the moral attributes of God, except very faintly. Design teaches me power, skill and goodness—not sanctity, not mercy, not a future judgment, which three are of the essence of religion."[25]

Newman's whole approach to the great questions of religion is personal and concrete. It is by personal influence that the truth is spread. For that, the deepest conviction is necessary. Truth is attained by the whole person, the whole moral being, and not by a mere passive reception of arguments. Most important of all, religion is a personal relationship with the Divine Being. Ever since his first conversion Newman has seen the *meaning* of loving God. The outlook of his heroine, Callista, well expresses this mutual love. As to philosophy, it dwelt only in conjecture and opinion; whereas the very essence of religion was, she felt, a recognition of the worshippers on the part of the Object of it. Religion could not be without hope. To worship a being who did not speak to us, recognise us, love us, was not religion. It might be a duty, it might be a merit; but her instinctive notion of religion was the soul's response to a God who had taken notice of the soul. It was loving intercourse. . . the intimate Divine Presence in the heart. It was the friendship or mutual love of person with person.[26]

In one of his earliest printed sermons Newman describes the unfolding of this personal relationship with God:

> To understand that we have souls, is to feel our separation from things visible, our independence of them, our distinct existence in ourselves, our individuality, our power of acting for ourselves in this way or that way, our accountableness for what we do. These are the great truths which lie wrapped up indeed even in a child's mind, and which God's grace can unfold there in spite of the influence of the external world; but at first this outward world prevails. We look off from self to the things around us, and forget ourselves in them. Such is our state—a depending for support on the reeds which are no stay, and overlooking our real strength—at the time when God begins his process of reclaiming us to a truer view of our place in his great system of providence.

The world begins to disappoint us. "We still crave for something, we know not well what; but we are sure it is something which the world has not given us." The world keeps changing, and

> We feel that, while it changes, we are one and the same; and thus, under God's blessing, we come to have some glimpse of the meaning of our independence of things temporal, and our immortality. And should it so happen that misfortunes come upon us (as they often do), then still more are we led to understand the nothingness of this world; then still more are we led to distrust it, and are weaned from the love of it, till at length it floats before our eyes merely as some idle veil, which, notwithstanding its many tints, cannot hide the view of what is beyond it; and we begin, by degrees, to perceive that there are but two beings in the whole universe, our own soul, and the God who made it.[27]

This was an echo of what Newman had learned at his first conversion, when he was led to "rest in the thought of two and two only luminously self-evident beings, myself and my Creator." It was an echo, too, of the whole Christian ascetical tradition, from the Fathers of the desert down, who sought to live with God alone. As St Gregory says of St Benedict, "solus in superni Spectatoris oculis habitavit secum".[28] Later we have St Teresa telling us in her *Life*, "the utmost we have to do at first is to take care of our soul, and to remember that in the entire world there is only God and the soul." St John of the Cross gives the same advice, "Live in the world as though there were in it but God and thy soul."

With this vivid realisation of God's presence there goes in Newman an equally vivid realisation of his particular Providence. It was this vivid sense of God's individual care which kept him serene in the many trials and anxieties of his life. It flowed from his concrete, personal approach to God and to religion. It is part of the faith of a Christian, and it enables us to persevere in our personal apostolate, in spite of apparent failure. In the sermon "A Particular Providence as Revealed in the Gospel" Newman describes it:

> If we allow ourselves to float down the current of the world, living as other men, gathering up our notions of religion here and there, as it may be, we have little or no true comprehension of a particular Providence. We conceive that Almighty God works on a large plan; but we cannot realise the wonderful truth that he sees and thinks of individuals. . . We cannot bring ourselves to get hold of the solemn fact, that he sees what is going on among ourselves at this moment; that this man falls and that man is exalted, at his silent, invisible appointment.

Newman then goes on to illustrate God's particular Providence by means of the tenderness and considerateness of our Lord in the Gospel. From our Maker's being invisible, and from the very extent and complication of the world's system, our imagination has great difficulty in attributing these qualities to him, even when our reason is convinced, and we wish to do so. Our Lord's behaviour towards his apostles brings the truth home to us. And Newman concludes that while the multitude may be insensible, "men of keener hearts would be overpowered by despondency, and would even loathe existence, did they suppose themselves under the mere operation of fixed laws, powerless to excite the pity or the attention of him who has appointed them."[29]

In an essay, Newman describes how this can be:

> All God's dealings with his creatures have two aspects, one external, one internal. . . This is the law of Providence here below; it works beneath a veil, and what is visible in its course does but shadow out at most, and sometimes obscures and

disguises what is invisible. The world in which we are placed has its own system of laws and principles, which, as far as knowledge goes, is, when once set in motion, sufficient to account for itself —as complete and independent as if there was nothing beyond it. . . The sun rises and sets on a law; the earth is covered with verdure or buried in the ocean, it grows old and it grows young again, by the operation of fixed laws. . . Men grow to maturity and then decay and die. Moreover, they form into society, and society has its principles. . . And these laws of the social and political world run into the physical, making all that is seen one and one only system; a horse stumbles, and an oppressed people is rid of their tyrant; a volcano changes prosperous cities into a dull lake. . . We cannot set limits either to the extent or the minuteness of this wonderful web of causes and effects, in which all we see is involved. It reaches to the skies; it penetrates into our very thoughts, habits, and will.

Such is confessedly the world in which our Almighty Creator has placed us. If then he is still actively present with his own work, present with nations and with individuals, he must be acting by means of his ordinary system, or by quickening, or as it were stimulating its powers, or by superseding or interrupting it; in other words, by means of what is called nature, or by miracle; and whereas strictly miraculous interference must be, from the nature of the case, rare, it stands to reason that, unless he has simply retired, and has left the world ordinarily to itself, content with having originally imposed on it certain laws. . . he is acting through, with, and beneath those physical, and social and moral laws, of which our experience informs us. Now it has ever been a firm article of Christian faith, that his Providence is in fact not merely general, but is, on the contrary, thus particular and personal; and that, as there is a parti-

> cular Providence, so of necessity that Providence is secretly concurring and cooperating with that system which meets the eye, and which is commonly recognised among men as existing. It is not too much to say that this is the one great rule on which the Divine dispensations with mankind have been and are conducted, that the visible world is the instrument, yet the veil, of the world invisible—the veil, yet still partially the symbol and index: so that all that exists or happens visibly, conceals and yet suggests, and above all subserves, a system of persons, facts, and events beyond itself.[30]

After this, we understand how Newman could say elsewhere:

"Let a person who trusts he is on the whole serving God acceptably, look back upon his past life, and he will find how critical were moments and acts, which at the time seemed the most indifferent: as for instance the school he was sent to as a child, the occasion of his falling in with those persons who have most benefited him, the accidents which determined his calling or his prospects, whatever they were. God's hand is ever over his own, and he leads them forward by ways they know not of."[31]

What has to be said, then, about the pastor of souls is something very simple. The work of an apostle is to raise the dead, and it is done by personal influence, by the man who is utterly convinced of the Christian faith, filled with a sense of God's presence and of his loving individual Providence. This deep faith is attained by those who are faithful to the light of conscience, and it enables them to face the self-denial and sacrifice their work requires. In the case of those who possess it "heart speaks to heart". A handful of such men are sufficient to carry on God's noiseless work.

Newman was preaching to the prosperous educated

classes of England, nearly 150 years ago, when other-worldliness was hardly a danger. He had to deal with human nature in what is, surely, its normal state, where the unseen world seems far off and unreal, so that it is necessary to bring it urgently before men's minds. But he who thought of the Church as a communion, in which the laity was the more interesting part, never forgot their concrete situation. Life was for action, and his was lived in the world of men. He reminds us that: "It would be a great mistake for us to suppose that we need quit our temporal calling, and go into retirement, in order to serve God acceptably. Christianity is a religion for the world, for the busy and influential, as well as for the poor."[32] In the sermon "Doing glory to God in pursuits of the World" he says:

> When persons are convinced that life is short. . . when they feel that the next life is all in all, and that eternity is the only subject that really can claim or occupy our thoughts, then they are apt to undervalue this life altogether, and to forget its real importance. They are apt to wish to spend the time of their sojourning here in a positive separation from active and social duties: yet it should be recollected that the employments of this world though not themselves heavenly, are after all the way to heaven. . . but it is difficult to realise this. It is difficult to realise both truths at once, and to connect both truths together; steadily to contemplate the life to come, yet to act in this. . . In various ways does the thought of the next world lead men to neglect their duty in this; and whenever it does so we may be sure that there is something wrong and unChristian, not in their thinking of the next world, but in their manner of thinking of it.

And Newman goes on to say:

> The Christian will feel that the true contemplation of his Saviour lies *in* his worldly business; that as

> Christ is seen in the poor, and in the persecuted, and in children, so he is seen in the employments which he puts upon his chosen, whatever they be; that in attending to his own calling he will be meeting Christ; that if he neglect it, he will not on that account enjoy his presence at all the more, but that while performing it, he will see Christ revealed to his soul amid the ordinary actions of the day, as by a sort of sacrament.[33]

Nor is grace to be separated from nature. Newman remarks of St Paul's gift of sympathy: "Wonderful to say, he who had rest and peace in the love of Christ, was not satisfied without the love of men; he whose supreme reward was the approbation of God, looked out for the approval of his brethren. . . He loved his brethren, not only 'for Jesus' sake', to use his own expression, but for their own sake also."[34] Newman certainly followed his own advice "that the best preparation for loving the world at large, and loving it duly and wisely, is to cultivate an intimate friendship and affection towards those who are immediately about us."[35]

In his sermons, too, he reminded men of their social duties and responsibilities and denounced unprincipled money-making, but, as he wrote to a friend in 1883: "It has never been my line to take up political or social questions, unless they came close to me as matters of personal duty." His was always the personal approach, and what appalled him was heartless treatment. He devoted much time to visiting and caring for the poor when they came under his charge at Oxford, Littlemore, and Birmingham. He paid, too for his brother's education, and provided for his mother and sisters, when the family fortunes declined.

The direct remedying of social ills, he would no doubt have said, lay with the statesmen and qualified administrators. Newman was preoccupied with the fundamental spiritual problems, the right solution of which has more to do even with immediate human happiness than more tangible social reforms. The decline in religious belief was a social problem of the first order, indeed the deepest of all social problems. Since Newman's day men have learned what cruelty and tyranny can follow, when the sacred character of the human person and the absolute value of the human soul are forgotten or denied. The present disarray in the prosperous western world is caused much less by social injustice than by the hankering after a purpose in life, in fact by a hunger for God.

This brings us back to where we began, how are we to spread to others the Gospel Truth? By our personal influence, flowing from our utter conviction of God's presence and loving care. As Newman says at the end of his sermon "Unreal Words":

> It is not an easy thing to learn that new language which Christ has brought us. He has interpreted all things for us in a new way; he has brought us a religion which sheds a new light on all that happens. Try to learn this language. Do not get it by rote, or speak it as a thing of course. Try to understand what you say. Time is short, eternity is long; God is great, man is weak; he stands between heaven and hell; Christ is his Saviour; Christ has suffered for him. The Holy Ghost sanctifies him; repentance purifies him, faith justifies, works save. These are solemn truths, which need not be actually spoken, except in the way of creed or of teaching; but which must be laid up in the heart. That a thing is true, is no reason that it should be said, but that it should be done; that it should be acted upon; that it should be made our own inwardly.[36]

3 Christ hidden

At the beginning of his sermon "Christ hidden from the World" Newman notices how when our Lord came on earth, he went unrecognised. Men came close to him, and did not know who he was. The light shone in the darkness, and darkness did not comprehend. This was true not only of enemies but of our Lord's own family, who seem to have thought him out of his mind, and of his disciples. "Have I been so long with you, and yet you do not know me, Philip?" Only gradually and not until after the Resurrection did the apostles fully believe.

This leads to the very serious thought that if Christ were near us and we did not see anything wonderful in him, this might be a clear proof that we were not his, for "his sheep know his voice and follow him". Many people, including the soldiers who crucified him, came very close to our Lord without realising who he was. And he remains hidden still. True believers have him spiritually within them. The Church is his Body. "Why persecutest thou me?" He is in the poor and suffering. "Inasmuch as you did it to the least of my brethren, you did it to me." The Corinthians were blamed for "not discerning the Body of the Lord".

With Newman as our guide, let us try to recognise Christ, who is hidden from the world. Not that Newman has anything new to say. He did not wish to preach any other Gospel than that which we have received. In a revealed religion what matters is to preserve the tradition. He has no special spirituality of his own, but he puts forward the age-long truth in a way that enables us to realise better who Christ is. He reminds us that "Christianity is eminently an objective religion. For the most part it tells us of persons and facts in simple words, and leaves that announcement to produce its effects on such hearts as are prepared to receive it."[1]

In *The Development of Christian Doctrine* Newman considers "the Incarnation the central truth of the Gospel, and the source whence we are to draw out its principles. This great doctrine is unequivocally announced in numberless passages of the New Testament 'The Word was made flesh and dwelt among us, full of grace and truth'. . . 'though he was rich, yet for your sakes he became poor', etc. In such passages as these Newman continues, "we have:

> 1) The principle of *dogma*, that is supernatural truths irrevocably committed to human language, imperfect because it is human, but definitive and necessary because given from above.
>
> 2) The principle of *faith*, which is the correlative of dogma, being the absolute acceptance of the divine word with an internal assent, in opposition to the informations, if such, of sight and reason.
>
> 3) Faith, being an act of the intellect, opens a way for inquiry, comparison and inference, that is, for science in religion. . . this is the principle of *theology*.
>
> 4) The doctrine of the Incarnation is the announcement of a divine gift conveyed in a material and visible medium, it being thus that heaven and earth are in the Incarnation united. That is, it establishes in the very idea of Christianity the *sacramental* principle as its characteristic.
>
> 5) Another principle involved in the doctrine of the Incarnation. . . is the necessary use of language. . . in a *mystical sense*. Words must be made to express new ideas, and are invested with a sacramental office.

6) It is our Lord's intention in his Incarnation to make us what he is himself; that is the principle of *grace*, which is not only holy but sanctifying.

7) It cannot elevate and change us without mortifying our lower nature. Here is the principle of *asceticism.*

8) And involved in this death of the natural man, is necessarily a revelation of the *malignity of sin*, in corroboration of the forebodings of conscience.

9) Also by the fact of an Incarnation we are taught that matter is an essential part of us, and, as well as mind, is *capable of sanctification.*[2]

Newman goes on to show how these principles are "as patent and operative, in the Latin and Greek Christianity of this day, as they were in the beginning". He felt it necessary to preach the central truth on which they are based, when the Oxford Movement was at its zenith, and his words have undoubtedly a value for us in the Catholic Church, 150 years later. Preaching in St Mary's, Oxford, Newman called the subject not abstract and speculative, but "essentially practical". And he continued:

> There is much in the religious belief, even of the more serious part of the community at present, to make observant men very anxious where it will end. It would be no very difficult matter, I suspect, to perplex the faith of a great many persons who believe themselves to be orthodox, and, indeed, are so, according to their light. They have been accustomed to call Christ God, but that is all; they have not considered what is meant by applying that title to one who was really a man. . . In truth, until we contemplate our Lord and Saviour, God and man, as a really existing being, external to our minds, as complete and entire in his personality as we show ourselves to be to each other, as one and the same in all his various and contrary attributes, "the same yesterday, today,

> and for ever", we are using words which profit not. Till then we do not realise that object of faith, which is not a mere name in which titles and properties may be affixed without congruity and meaning, but has a personal existence and an identity distinct from everything else. In what sense do we "know" him, if our idea of him be not such as to take up and incorporate into itself the manifold attributes and offices which we ascribe to him? What do we gain from words, however correct and abundant, if they end with themselves, instead of lighting up the image of the Incarnate Son on our hearts?

Newman continues that "we have well-nigh ceased to regard him, after the pattern of the Nicene Creed, as 'God from God, and Light from Light', ever one with him, yet ever distinct from him. . . He who was but now spoken of as God, without mention of the Father from whom he is, is next described as if a creature, but how do these distinct notions of him hold together in our minds?"[3]

Before considering how Newman answers his question, and how he unfolds the doctrine of the Son of God made man, it will be advisable to pause for a moment, and go back from the Economy to the Theology, from the Incarnation to the Most Holy Trinity. This can only be done briefly, but it will perhaps make the way forward easier.

In various places in his treatises and his sermons Newman was led to expound the doctrine of the Trinity, in *The Arians of the Fourth Century*, in *St Athanasius*, and in *Tracts Theological*. As might be expected, nowhere more than in this sphere was the influence of the Greek fathers on him so strong. As is well known, the starting point in Latin theology has been the idea of the eminent and absolute simplicity of the divine nature—that came first, and the idea of the distinction of persons was reduced in significance. In more recent years there has been a change, as the writings of Karl Rahner bear witness, but a hundred and fifty years ago Newman was carrying on in the West the eastern tradition, where Petaù had maintained it before him.

The Greek theology begins with the personal God, who is the Father, and who therefore has a Son, to whom he gives his nature. The Son *possesses* the same divine nature as the Father by way of consequence. Finally, God who is the Father has his Spirit who, proceeding from him, *receives* the same divine nature. This Spirit proceeds from the Father as Father, and so from the Father through the Son, and so possesses the same divine nature as Father and Son, in virtue of his procession.

Thus the Greek conception fixes first on the persons, begins with God who is a person, to go to others equally divine—the nature is seen in each person as possessing it. The persons have and give or receive what they have. The divine nature is not thought of first, it is consequential. The processions do not grow out of a unique nature, rather the unity of nature is the result of the procession of the persons.

Now let us hear Newman:

> Christianity began its teaching by denouncing polytheism as absurd and wicked; but the retort on the part of the polytheist was obvious: Christianity taught a divine Trinity: how was this consistent with its profession of monarchy? on the other hand, if there was a divine *Monarchia*, how was not Sabellius right in denying the distinction of persons in the divine essence? or, if not Sabellius, then Arius, who degraded Son and Spirit to the condition of creatures?. . . Catholic theologians met this difficulty, both before and after the Nicene Council, by insisting on the unity of origin, which they taught as existing in the Divine Triad, the Son and Spirit having a com-

> municated divinity from the Father, and a personal unity with him; the three persons being internal to the divine essence, unlike the polytheism of the Greeks and Romans.

Newman also quotes St Athanasius: "We preserve one origin of divinity, and not two origins, whence there is properly a monarch." Newman continues: "It was for the same reason that the Father was called God absolutely, while the second and third persons were designated by their personal names of 'the Son' or 'the Word', and 'the Holy Ghost'; because they are to be regarded, not as separated from, but as inherent in the Father."[4] This way of speaking has the support of Scripture, and of the nature of the case, since the notion of Father carries with it a claim to priority in the order of our ideas. Thus the early Fathers: "Instead of saying 'Father, Son and Spirit are one substance', they would say, 'In one God and Father are the Son and Spirit'; the words 'one Father' standing not only for the person of the Father, but connoting that sole divine substance which is one with his person."[5] This doctrine of the principatus of the Father was thrown into the background in the West on account of its abuse by the Arians, but Newman remarks: "However, what St Irenaeus, St Athanasius, and St Basil taught, never can be put aside. It is as true now as when those great Fathers enunciated it; and if true, it cannot be ignored without some detriment to the fullness and symmetry of the Catholic dogma."

The reason for describing it here is its relation to the mystery of the Son of God made man. As Newman says of the *Monarchia*:

> One obvious use of it is to facilitate to the imagination the descent of the divine nature to the human, as required in the doctrine of the Incarnation; the eternal Son of God becoming by a second birth the Son of God in time, is a line of thought which preserves to us the continuity of

> idea in the divine revelation; whereas if we say abruptly that the Supreme Being became the Son of Mary, this, however true when taken by itself, still by reason of the infinite distance between God and man, acts in the direction of the Nestorian error of a Christ with two persons, as certainly as the doctrine of the *Principatus*, when taken by itself, favours the Arian error of a merely human Christ.[6]

Our Lord is God because he is the Son of God. In the sermon "Christ the Son of God made Man", Newman explains:

> This, then, is the point of doctrine which I had to mention, that our Lord is not only God, but the Son of God. We know more than that God took on him our flesh; though all is mysterious, we have a point of knowledge further and more distinct, namely that it was neither the Father nor the Holy Ghost, but the Son of the Father, God the Son, God from God, and Light from Light, who came down on earth, and who thus, though graciously taking on him a new nature, remained in person as he had been from everlasting, the *Son* of the Father, and spoke and acted towards the Father as a Son.[7]

This last quotation leads on to this further point. It is the boast of the Eastern writers that the Orthodox Church "never considers the humanity of Christ in abstractions, apart from his Godhead, whose fulness dwells in him bodily". "This deified humanity always assumes for the Orthodox Christian that same glorious form under which it appeared to the disciples on Mount Tabor."[8] How true this is of Newman and the reverent way he always speaks of our Lord:

> We have well-nigh forgotten the sacred truth, graciously disclosed for our support, that Christ is the Son of God in his divine nature, as well as

> in his human. . . We speak of him in a vague way as God, which is true, but not the whole truth; and, in consequence, when we proceed to consider his humiliation, we are unable to carry on the notion of his personality from heaven to earth . . . but when we merely speak, first of God, then of man, we seem to change the nature without preserving the person. In truth his divine Sonship is that portion of the sacred doctrine, on which the mind is providentially intended to rest throughout, and so to preserve for itself his identity unbroken.[9]

With the Alexandrian Fathers Newman always insists on the unity of Christ, and defends the way they speak of there being only "one nature" in the Incarnate Son. He writes:

> The Divine Word was not a mere presence or manifestation of God in man, but he was God himself incarnate. He was still what he had ever been, and will be from first to last, One–one and the same, impassible, immutable, in his identity, so to speak, as being one of the eternal Trinity. His divine nature carried with it in his incarnation that identity or personality. So necessary, so cardinal is this truth for the right holding of the great doctrine under consideration, that the Alexandrians, St Cyril at least, and perhaps St Athanasius, spoke of there being only "one nature" in the Incarnate Lord, meaning thereby one person (for person and nature could not be divided; and, if our Lord's nature was divine, his person was divine also), and by saying "only one", was meant that in comparison of the divine person who had taken flesh, what he had taken was not so much a nature, (though it was strictly a nature) as the substance of a manhood which was not substantive.

The unity of Christ lies in his person, which brings

the two natures together, and which is and ever has been indivisible from his divine nature. From eternity the Son was in possession and in the fullness of his Godhead. And "when he became man, he lost nothing by becoming. All that he had ever been continued to be his; what he took on himself was only an addition. There was no change, he did but put on a garment."[10]

Hence Newman defends and explains the famous formula of St Cyril, of the Word's "One Nature Incarnate". "It is called one, in the first place because, even after the Incarnation, it and no other nature is, strictly speaking, *his own*, the flesh being taken on; in the second place because it, and no other, has been his from the first; and in the third place because it has ever been one and the same, in nowise affected as to its perfection by the Incarnation." Newman continues:

> It is called incarnate in order to express the dependence, subordination, and restriction of his humanity, which (1) has neither principle nor personality; (2) has no distinct sonship, though it involves a new generation; (3) is not possessed of the fullness of characterisitics which attached to any other specimen of our race. On which account, while it is recognised as a perfect nature, it may be spoken of as existing after the manner of an attribute rather than of a substantive being, which it really is.[11]

This is authentic Christian doctrine, although it is unpalatable to many who write on Christology today, without paying sufficient attention to the teachings of tradition. Newman and the Eastern writers are at one in upholding it. Anglicans, such as the great Oxford patristic scholar William Bright, have shared it. Criticising H. M. Gwatkin's *Studies in Arianism* he remarks: "Mr Gwatkin might have learned much from *The Arians of the Fourth Century*, if he had been more truly in sympathy with its interior spirit." Then to illustrate Newman's "peculiar combination of awe and tenderness" in dealing with his subject, Bright quotes from *The Arians in the Fourth Century*:

> More than enough has now been said in explanation of a controversy, the very sound of which must be painful to any one who has a loving faith in the divinity of the Son. Yet so it is ordered, that he who was once lifted up to the gaze of the world, and hid not his face from contumely, has again been subjected to rude scrutiny and dishonour in the promulgation of his religion to the world. And his true followers have been obliged in his defence to raise and fix their eyes boldly on him, as if he were one of themselves, dismissing the natural reverence, which would keep them ever at his feet.[12]

Bright then comments:

> How characteristic are these words! how well we know the thrill of their solemn music! how they illustrate what was said of Newman as "one who at favoured moments half lifted the veil of the unseen. . ." Nothing could be more pitiable than for a person to adopt such a tone as breathes through the above extract, unless it were natural to him. . . this tone, where it exists, does give a book or a speech a special and indescribable charm.[13]

But Newman submitted to revealed religion, and so his was a balanced doctrine. He presents Jesus Christ, truly man, as the Gospel portrays him. Dean Church in his account of the Oxford Movement remarked: "Evangelical theology had dwelt upon the work of Christ, and laid comparatively little stress on his example, or the picture left us of his personality and life. It regarded the Epistles of St Paul as the last word of the Gospel message." But now there was a change. "The great name no longer stood for an abstract symbol of doctrine, but for a living master, who could teach as well as save. . . It was a change in the look and use of scripture, which some can still look back to as an epoch in their religious history."[14]

Newman himself said in his sermon, "The Tears of Christ at the Grave of Lazarus":

> It is very much the fashion at present to regard the Saviour of the world in an irreverent and unreal way—as a mere idea or vision; to speak of him so narrowly and unfruitfully as if we only knew of his name; though scripture has set him before us in his actual sojourn on earth, in his gestures, words and deeds, in order that we may have that on which to fix our eyes. And till we learn to do this, to leave off vague statements about his love, his willingness to receive the sinner, his imparting repentance and spiritual aid and the like, and view him in his particular and actual works, set before us in scripture, surely we have not derived from the gospels that very benefit which they are intended to convey. Nay, we are in some danger, perhaps, even as regards our faith; for, it is to be feared, while the thought of Christ is but a creation of our minds, it may gradually change or fade away, it may become defective or perverted; whereas, when we contemplate Christ as manifested in the gospels, the Christ who exists therein, external to our own imaginings, and who is as really a living being, and sojourned on earth as truly as any of us, then we shall at length believe in him with a conviction, a confidence, and an entireness, which can no more be annihilated than the belief in our senses.[15]

In the same sermon, already quoted, in which Newman insisted so strongly on our Lord's Divinity, he also said:

> That eternal power, which until then has thought and acted as God, began to think and act as a man, with all man's faculties, affections, and

> imperfections, sin excepted. Before he came on earth he was infinitely above joy and grief, fear and anger, pain and heaviness; but afterwards all these properties and many more were his as fully as they are ours. Before he came on earth, he had but the perfections of God, but afterwards he had also the virtues of a creature, such as faith, meekness, self-denial. Before he came on earth he could not be tempted of evil; but afterwards he had a man's heart, a man's tears, and a man's wants and infirmities. His divine nature indeed pervaded his manhood, so that every deed and word of his in the flesh savoured of eternity and infinity; but, on the other hand, from the time he was born of the Virgin Mary, he had a natural fear of danger, a natural shrinking from pain, though ever subject to the ruling influence of that holy and eternal essence which was in him.[16]

Again: "There is not a feeling, not a passion, not a wish, not an infirmity, which we have, which did not belong to that manhood which he assumed, except such as is of the nature of sin. There was not a trial or temptation which befalls us, but was, in kind at least, presented before him, except that he had nothing within him, sympathising with that which came to him from without."[17] So truly was he man that he was hidden from the world. As we saw at the beginning, he came to his own, but they did not recognise him.

In one of his Meditations, written when an Oratorian, Newman prayed:

> Thou wouldst not come in any shape or capacity or office which was above the course of ordinary human life–not as a Nazarene, not as a Levitical priest, not as a monk, not as a hermit, but in the fullness and exactness of that human nature which so much thou lovest. Thou camest not only a perfect man, but as a proper man. . . Thou art more fully man than the holy Baptist, than St

> John, Apostle and Evangelist, than thy own sweet Mother. As in divine knowledge of me thou art beyond them all, so also in experience and personal knowledge of my nature. Thou art my elder brother. How can I fear, how should I not repose my whole heart on one so gentle, so tender, so familiar, so unpretending, so modest, so natural, so humble? Thou art now, though in heaven, just the same as thou wast on earth: the mighty God, yet the little child—the all-holy, yet the all-sensitive, all-human.[18]

Although clear and balanced in his enunciations Newman always preserves the sense of the mystery in Christianity. He has a deep sense of reverence, and of the divine transcendence. He complained of the Arians that "They did not admit into their theology the notion of mystery. . . It was useless to urge on them that they were reasoning about matters upon which they had no experimental knowledge."[19] In his book *The Arians* he emphasised that "the meaning and practical results of deep-seated religious reverence were far better understood in the primitive times than now, when the infidelity of the world has corrupted the Church. Now, we allow ourselves publicly to canvass the most solemn truths in a careless or fiercely argumentative way."

Also, "there is that in religious mysteries which is ever distasteful to secular minds. . . what at once demands attention, yet refuses to satisfy curiosity, places itself above the human mind, imprints on it the thought of him who is eternal, and enforces the necessity of obedience for its own sake. And thus it becomes to the proud and irreverent, what the consciousness of guilt is to the sinner: a spectre haunting the field, and disturbing the complacency, of their intellectual investigations."[20]

Newman insists "that mystery is the necessary note of divine revelation, that is, mystery subjectively to the human mind; because, when the mind goes on freely to reason from language that only partially corresponds to eternal truths, and which cannot be adequately expressed in words, it draws from one revealed information what is inconsistent with what it draws from another, and ought to say 'This collision of deductions arises from the imperfection of our knowledge.'"[21]

All this was especially true of the doctrine of the atonement, so dissected and rationalised in the West, and used so crudely by the evangelicals of the day. It was so often used "as the *one* doctrine to be addressed to all". This Newman thought very irreverent. It "would excite the feelings rather than mend the heart".[22] He insists that we are dealing with a mystery, to be accepted on faith.

> For though the death of Christ manifests God's *hatred of sin*, as well as his love for man, (inasmuch as it was sin that made his death necessary, and the greater the sacrifice the greater must have been the evil that caused it), yet *how* his death expiated our sins, and what satisfaction it was to God's *justice*, are surely subjects quite above us. It is in no way a great and glorious *manifestation* of his justice. . . as explaining in what way it satisfied; it is an event ever *mysterious* on account of its necessity, while it is *fearful* from the hatred of sin implied in it, and most *transporting and elevating* from its display of God's love to man.[23]

That was said when an Anglican, and as a Catholic he said the same. Our Lord's suffering was voluntary.

> He came to die when he need not have died; he died to satisfy for what he might have pardoned without satisfaction; he paid a price which need not have been asked, nay, which needed to be accepted when paid. It may be said with truth that, rigorously speaking, one being can never, by his own suffering, simply discharge the debt

> of another's sin. Accordingly, he died, not in order to exert a peremptory claim on the divine justice, if I may so speak—as if he were bargaining in the market place, or pursuing a plea in a court of law—but in a more generous, munificent way, did he shed that blood. . . in accordance with *his* Father's will, who, for wise reasons unrevealed, exacted it.[24]

The breadth of Newman's view is further brought out in his account of the teaching of St Ignatius of Antioch, which he makes his own. Our salvation lies not in the atonement by itself, but in the incarnation. "But neither in the incarnation nor atonement as past events, but as present facts, in an existing mode, in which our Saviour comes to us; or, to speak more plainly, in our Saviour himself, who is God in our flesh, and not only so, but in flesh that has been offered up on the Cross in sacrifice, which has died and has risen. The being made man, the being crucified in atonement, the being raised again, are the three past events" thanks to which our Lord has become our Saviour, "and those who omit the resurrection in their view of the divine economy, are as really defective in faith as if they omitted the crucifixion."

Our Lord could not apply his atonement without rising again. We are saved by the flesh and blood of the risen Lord, first sacrificed for us, then communicated to us. St Ignatius, and after him the Catholic Church teaches "that the *body* and *blood* of the Word incarnate is in some real, though unknown way, communicated to our souls and bodies, and thus becomes the principle of a new life". When Ignatius speaks of a "union with the flesh and spirit of Jesus Christ", and of our "possessing an indivisible Spirit, which is Jesus Christ", he speaks of union with Christ's *flesh*, which is *spirit.*[25] Hence "as we know nothing of the atonement except as wrought through Christ's natural body, so we know nothing of justification except as wrought through his mystical".[26]

At the risk of anticipating what has to be developed later, it is necessary to call attention to the part Christ in his mystical body plays in the work of our redemption.

There is this passage in the sermon "The Communion of Saints":

> Christ formed his apostles into a visible society; but when he came again in the person of his Spirit, he made them all in a real sense one, not in name only. For they were no longer arranged merely in the form of unity, as the limbs of the dead may be, but they were parts and organs of one unseen power; they really depended upon and were offshoots of that which was one; their separate persons were taken into a mysterious union with things unseen, were grafted upon and assimilated to the spiritual body of Christ, which is one, even by the Holy Ghost, in whom Christ has come again to us. Thus Christ came, not to make us one, but to die for us: the Spirit came to make us one in him who had died and was alive, that is to form the Church. This then is the special glory of the Christian Church, that its members do not depend merely on what is visible, they are not mere stones of a building, piled one on another, and bound together from without, but they are one and all the births and manifestations of one and the same unseen spiritual principle or power, "living stones", internally connected, as branches from a tree, not as the parts of a heap. They are members of the body of Christ. That divine and adorable form, which the apostles saw and handled, after ascending into heaven became a principle of life, a secret origin of existence to all who believe, through the gracious ministration of the Holy Ghost. . . So that in a true sense it may be said, that from the day of Pentecost to this hour there has been in the Church but one Holy One, the King of Kings,

> the Lord of lords himself, who is in all believers, and through whom they are what they are; their separate persons being but as separate developments, vessels, instruments, and works of him who is invisible. Such is the difference between the Church before the Spirit of Christ came, and after. Before, God's servants were as the dry bones of the Prophet's vision, connected by profession, not by an inward principle; but since, they are all the organs as if of one invisible, governing soul, the hands, or the tongues, or the feet, or the eyes of one and the same directing mind, the types, tokens, beginnings, and glimpses of the eternal Son of God.[27]

The thought of the Mystical Body leads on to that other Mystical Body, the eucharist. Here is the Catholic doctrine, which Newman was preaching quite early in the Oxford Movement, in his sermon, "Christ a Quickening Spirit":

> We must not suppose that on leaving us he closed the gracious economy of his incarnation, and withdrew the ministration of his incorruptible manhood from his work of loving mercy towards us. . . Before he went away, he remembered our necessity, and completed his work, bequeathing to us a special mode of approaching him, a holy mystery, in which we receive (we know not how) the virtue of that heavenly body which is the life of all who believe. This is the blessed sacrament of the eucharist, in which "Christ is evidently set forth crucified among us"; that we, feasting upon the sacrifice, may be "partakers of the Divine Nature". Let us give heed lest we be in the number of those who "discern not the Lord's Body", and the "exceeding great and precious promises" which are made to those who partake it. . . Blessed are they beyond language or thought, to whom it is vouchsafed to receive those tokens of his love, which cannot be otherwise gained by man, the

> pledges and means of his special presence, in the sacrament of his supper; who are allowed to eat and drink the food of immortality, and receive life from the bleeding side of the Son of God![28]

In the sermon "The Eucharistic Presence" Newman speaks like Odo Casel about the sacrament of holy communion: "Christ who died and rose again for us, is in it spiritually present, in the fullness of his death and of his resurrection." And he goes on to explain: "We call his presence in this holy sacrament a spiritual presence, not as if 'spiritual' were but a name or mode of speech, and he were really absent, but by way of expressing that he who is present there can neither be seen nor heard; that he cannot be ascertained or approached by any of the senses; that he is not present in place, that he is not present carnally, though he is really present."[29]

Speaking of the sacraments, Newman says of Christ that:

> Though he now sits on the right hand of God, he has in one sense, never left the world since he first entered it; for by the ministration of the Holy Ghost, he is really present with us in an unknown way, and ever imparts himself to those who seek him. . . And as he is still with us, for all that he is in heaven, so, again, is the hour of his cross and passion ever mystically present, though it be past these eighteen hundred years. Time and space have no portion in the spiritual kingdom which he has founded; and the rites of his Church are as mysterious spells by which he annuls them both. . . Thus Christ shines through them, as through transparent bodies, without impediment. He is the light and life of the Church, acting through it, dispensing of his fullness, knitting and compacting together every part of it.[30]

It is not surprising, after this, to learn that Newman introduced a weekly communion service at St Mary's,

Oxford, and that the custom of more frequent celebrations began to spread.

In the texts already quoted, it will be noticed how Newman stresses communion as the act by which the individual Christian appropriates the grace of redemption, but his linking it so closely with the mystical body shows that he was far from forgetting the corporate nature of the holy eucharist. Coming together for worship is not a mere practical necessity, the rites which convey grace are committed to the *body* of Christians. The sacraments, baptism and the eucharist are social and public by their very nature, baptism as incorporating us in Christ's mystical body, and still more holy communion. "And hence it is," says Newman, "that so much stress is to be laid on the duty of united worship; for thus the multitude of believers coming together claim as one man the grace which is poured out upon the one undivided body of Christ mystical."[31]

"And further, it is to this one body, regarded as one, that the special privileges of the Gospel are given. It is not that this man receives the blessing, and that man, but one and all, the whole body as one man, one new spiritual man, with one accord, seeks and gains it."[32]

The same is true of prayer. "Nor could it be otherwise," says Newman, "if Christianity be a social religion, as it is pre-eminently. If Christians are to live together, they will pray together; and united prayer is necessarily of an intercessory character, as being offered for each other and for the whole, and for self as one of the whole. In proportion, then, as unity is an especial gospel-duty, so does gospel-prayer partake of a social character."[33]

Newman's, then, is a balanced doctrine, which does not forget the corporate nature of salvation. But, of course, the mystical body itself is composed of persons, and the supreme lesson of the Gospel is the union of each member individually with the head. Here is a quotation from the sermon on "Saving Knowledge":

> St John speaks of knowing Christ and of keeping his commandments, as the two great departments of religious duty and blessedness. To know Christ is to discern the Father of all, as manifested through his only-begotten Son incarnate. In the natural world we have glimpses, frequent and startling of his glorious attributes. . . but. . . they do not allow us in any comfortable sense to know God. . . And thus the gospels, which contain the memorials of this wonderful grace, are our principal treasures. They may be called the text of the revelation; and the epistles, especially St Paul's, are as comments upon it, unfolding and illustrating it in its various parts, raising history into doctrine, ordinances into sacraments, detached words or actions into principles, and thus everywhere dutifully preaching his person, work and will.[34]

Newman adds that the Creeds "speak of no ideal being, such as the imagination alone contemplates, but of the very Son of God, whose life is recorded in the gospels."[35] Elsewhere he explains how the Holy Spirit first inspired the evangelists, and then "commented (as it were) upon these, and unfolded their meaning in the apostolic epistles. The birth, the life, the death and resurrection of Christ, has been the text which he has illuminated. He has made history to be doctrine."[36]

An exposition of the supreme Christian privilege of our union with Christ comes in Newman's discussion of the teaching of St Athanasius:

> Our Lord, by becoming man, has found a way whereby to sanctify that nature of which his own manhood is the pattern specimen. He inhabits us personally, and this inhabitation is effected by the channel of the Sacraments. . . By this indwelling our Lord is the immediate *arché* (first principle) of spiritual life to each of his elect individually. . . It is plain that there is a special presence of God in those who are real members of our Lord. . .

> soul and body became, by the indwelling of the Word, so elevated above their natural state, so sacred, that to profane them is a sacrilege.[37]

With this most elevated truth we reach the heart of the Christian revelation. How did it affect Newman himself? Undoubtedly it underlay his lifelong serenity amid so many trials. With his sense of reverence and his reserve, he had a horror of any display in matters so sacred. Occasionally we have a suggestion of how he was affected. In a sermon of 1838, when the Oxford Movement was at its height, he speaks of Christ's presence through the sacraments:

> A thick black veil is spread between this world and the next. . . There is no access through it into the next world. In the Gospel this veil is not removed; it remains, but every now and then marvellous disclosures are made to us of what is behind it. At times we seem to catch a glimpse of a form which we shall hereafter see face to face. We approach, and in spite of the darkness, our hands, or our head, or our brow, or our lips become, as it were sensible of the contact of something more than earthly. We know not where we are, but we have been bathing in water, and a voice tells us that it is blood. Or we have a mark signed upon our foreheads, and it spake of Calvary. Or we recollect a hand laid upon our heads, and surely it had the print of the nails in it, and resembled his who with a touch gave sight to the blind and raised the dead. Or we have been eating and drinking; and it was not a dream surely, that one fed us from his wounded side, and renewed our nature by the heavenly meat he gave.[38]

No wonder the Catholic Newman could tell the Anglican disciples he was urging to follow him into the Catholic Church, that they had no need to deny the graces they had received through Anglican sacraments: "Can I wipe out from my memory or wish to wipe out, those happy Sunday mornings, light or dark, year after year, when I celebrated your communion-rite in my own church of St Mary's; and in the pleasantness and joy of it heard nothing of the strife of tongues which surrounded its walls?"[39]

In *Callista* Newman makes St Cyprian explain:

> We have no love for him who alone lasts. We love those things which do not last but come to an end. Things being thus, he whom we ought to love has determined to win us back to him. With this object he has come into his own world, in the form of one of us men. And in that human form he opens his arms and woos us to return to him, our maker. This is our worship, this is our love, Callista. . . There is but one lover of souls, cried Caecilius, and he loves each one of us, as though there were no one else to love. He died for each one of us, as if there were no one else to die for. He died on the shameful cross. "Amor meus crucifixus est." The love which he inspires lasts, for it is the love of the unchangeable. It satisfies, for he is inexhaustible. The nearer we draw to him, the more triumphantly does he enter into us; the longer he dwells in us, the more intimately we have possession of him. It is an espousal for eternity.[40]

In one of his Catholic meditations, published only after his death, Newman prays to our Lord:

> And now thou biddest me love thee in turn, for thou hast loved me. Thou wooest me to love thee specially, above others. . . Have I not cause to love thee abundantly more than others, though all ought to love thee? I do not know what thou hast done for others personally, though thou hast died for all—but I know what thou hast done especially for me. Thou hast done that for me, O my love, which ought to make me love thee with all my powers.[41]

There we catch a glimpse of Newman's love for Christ. This is how he sums up the duty of a Christian apostle:

> When men are to be exhorted to newness of life, the true object to be put before them, as I conceive, is "Jesus Christ, the same yesterday, today, and for ever"; the true Gospel preaching is to enlarge, as they can bear it, on the person, natures, attributes, offices, and work of him who once regenerated them, and is now ready to pardon; to dwell upon his recorded words and deeds on earth; to declare reverently and adoringly his mysterious greatness as the only-begotten Son, one with the Father, yet distinct from him; of him, yet not apart from him; eternal yet begotten; a Son, yet as if a servant; and to combine and to contrast his attributes and relations to us as God and man, as our mediator, saviour, sanctifier, and judge. The true preaching of the Gospel is to preach Christ.[42]

4 The indwelling Spirit

Newman begins his sermon "Contracted views in religion"[1] with an account of the elder brother in the parable, and his father's reply to him. "Son, thou art always with me. Why this sudden fear and distrust?" The son was disconcerted and angry, and this shows that in religion we need to guard against narrowness of mind, and the supposition that we have a clear knowledge of God's ways. We become over confident in our knowledge of God's ways, whereas we should always be learners in the school of divine truth, always ready to submit ourselves to the Christian revelation.

A striking example of a contracted view has been the attitude in the Western Church towards our Lord's resurrection, which was chiefly considered from the apologetic angle. Newman shares to the full the emphasis on the doctrine so well preserved in the East, of the saving value of the resurrection. In the consciousness of the West as it was before the Second Council of the Vatican, Easter seemed to have lost its central place. How little was heard of the paschal mystery, and what lavish praise was heaped on the books of Père Durrwell, on the ground that they remedied the current defective Catholic theology of the resurrection as a mystery of Salvation. Well over a century earlier Newman's sermons are full of the subject, of the day inaugurated by the resurrection, of the presence of Christ in his Church.

In the sermon on that subject he says: "The day, then, that dawned upon the Church at the resurrection, and beamed forth in full splendour at the ascension, that day which has no setting. . . in which we now are, is described in these words of Christ as a state of special divine manifestation, of special introduction into the presence of God. . . Thus we Christians stand in the courts of God most high, and in one sense, see his face."[2] And again: "We are able to see that the saviour, when once he entered into this world, never so departed as to suffer things to be as before he came; for he is still with us, not in mere gifts, but by the substitution of his Spirit for himself, and that both in the Church and in the souls of individual Christians."[3]

Newman deals with the subject *ex professo* in the ninth of his *Lectures on Justification*, "Righteousness the fruit of our Lord's resurrection." Here are some of his remarks: "In saying that Christ *rose again* for our justification, it is implied that justification is through that second Comforter who after the resurrection came down from heaven." Thus,

> Christ's work of mercy has two chief parts; what he did for all men, what he does for each; what he did once for all, what he does for one by one continually; what he did externally to us, what he does within us; what he did on earth, what he does in heaven; what he did in his own person, what he does by his Spirit; his death, and the blood and water after it; his meritorious sufferings, and the various gifts thereby purchased, of pardon, grace, reconciliation, renewal, holiness, spiritual communion; that is his atonement, and the application of his atonement, or his atonement and our justification; he atones by the offering of himself on the Cross; and as certainly (which is the point before us) he justifies by the mission of his Spirit.[4]

And again:

> He came once, then he ascended, he has come again. He came first in the flesh; he has come a

> second time in the Spirit. . . As in God's counsels it was necessary for the atonement that there should be a material, local, sacrifice of the Son once for all: so for our individual justification, there must be a spiritual, ubiquitous communication of that sacrifice continually. There was but one atonement; there are ten thousand justifications.[5]

And later again:

> Further, it would appear as if his going to his Father was, in fact, the same thing as his coming to us spiritually. I mean there is some mysterious unknown connection between his departing in his own person, and his returning in the person of his Spirit. He said that unless he went, his Spirit would not come to us. . . And thus his rising again was the necessary antecedent of his applying to his elect the virtue of that atonement which his dying wrought for all men. . . He died to purchase what he rose again to apply. "He died for our sins; he rose again for our justification." . . . He atoned I repeat, in his own person; he justified through his Spirit. And here I have touched upon another part of the harmony of the divine dispensation which may be profitably dwelt upon. For he himself was raised again and "justified" by the Spirit; and what was wrought in him is repeated in us who are his brethren, and the complement and ratification of his work. What took place in him as an origin, is continued on in the succession of those who inherit his fullness, and is the cause of its continuance.[6]

What we are told of the saving value of the Lord's resurrection leads on at once to his gift of the Holy Spirit, who dwells in the souls of the just and deifies them. Such is the plan of salvation. The first thing to be said about Newman's understanding of the doctrine of the indwelling in the soul of the Holy Spirit, and through him of the Father and the Son, is that it lay at the foundation of his religious life from the time of his first conversion as a boy.

It is very significant that this should have been the case, as showing how authentic his Christianity was; the dogma of the indwelling of the Blessed Trinity in the soul and that which attributes a special sanctifying action to the Holy Spirit being of such vital importance for anyone who would lead a truly Christian life. Indeed they are the culminating point of the Christian Revelation, whether considered historically or arranged schematically. These truths were the inspiration and support of Newman during the whole of his long career, until he went from shadows and images *in veritatem*.

Of the books given to Newman by Walter Mayers, the master at Ealing School, the most important were those of Thomas Scott, "the writer", Newman tells us in the *Apologia*, "who made a deeper impression on my mind than any other, and to whom (humanly speaking) I almost owe my soul."[7]

In his *Essays* Newman found the texts from St John and St Paul on the indwelling of the Holy Trinity clearly set out and emphasised, while Scott laments that so "many nominal Christians utterly disclaim all dependence on the Spirit as enthusiasm: and how greatly this part of the Gospel is overlooked by numbers who are zealous for other doctrines of it."[8] We still have prayers for the gift of the Holy Spirit which Newman composed at this time. In October 1817, at the beginning of his first term at Oxford, there is a prayer to Almighty God: "to give me thy Holy Spirit. Unto him who cleanseth the thoughts of our hearts, who maketh our bodies the temples of God, the blessed, holy, and eternal Spirit, to him be worship for ever".[9]

Then in one of his earliest sermons he says: "We are indeed as constantly and unceasingly dependent on the Holy Ghost for our heavenly life, as we are on the air around us for our natural life."[10] Yet, although Newman was living the doctrine, his mentions of it were sparing. One with his sense of reverence was not tempted to bring forward so sacred a doctrine, while he was still so young, and had no special call to do so, before an audience that was perhaps not prepared for it.

But as the Oxford Movement began the situation altered. Then the fullness of the Christian revelation was being rediscovered and Newman was faced with the practical necessity of providing a theological basis for the piety of his followers. How could he look for any other foundation than the one laid in the New Testament, for that new life of union with God, which the Christian religion offered to mankind? With his intimate knowledge of Holy Scripture, now reinforced by a profound study of the Fathers, Newman inevitably turned to the most precious part of our Lord's teaching, given at the most solemn moment of his life, as recorded by St John, and as preached by St Paul. Many long passages in *Parochial and Plain Sermons* are little more than extracts from those two writers. In the sermons not yet published of this period there is naturally more to be gleaned, but the full Catholic doctrine is set out at length, in many places, in a way never surpassed elsewhere, in *Parochial and Plain Sermons* and in *Lectures on Justification* of 1838.

In addition to this doctrine of the indwelling of the Blessed Trinity in the Christian being the revealed foundation of the spiritual life, Newman was drawn to it by his whole bent and character, the personal, concrete approach, "*Cor ad cor loquitur*". He could never have been satisfied with thinking of grace merely as a quality in the soul, a forgiveness of sin, or a strengthening force. Before his first conversion he said that he did not "see the *meaning* of loving God",[11] and after it, "that God gave me opportunities of loving him then". Nothing but union with God could satisfy.

"The philosopher aspires towards a divine *principle*," says Newman in the second University Sermon, "the Christian towards a Divine Agent", and "even the principle of good, when implanted and progressively realised in our hearts, is still continually revealed to us as a person, as if to mark strongly that it is not our own, and must lead us to no preposterous self-adoration." For instance, we read of Christ being formed in us—dwelling in the heart—of the Holy Spirit making us his temple; particularly remarkable is our Saviour's own promise: "If a man love me he will keep my words; and my Father will love him, and we will come unto him, and make our abode with him."[12]

If we are to summarise Newman's exposition of the Catholic doctrine we must begin by noting his emphasis on the need of reverence in treating of it, and his insistence that it is a hidden gift, known by faith. In the sermon for Pentecost "The Indwelling Spirit", he explains what this means, and adds:

> Such is the great doctrine which we hold as a matter of faith and without actual experience to verify it in us. Next I must speak briefly concerning the manner in which the gift of grace manifests itself in the regenerate soul, a subject which I do not willingly take up, and which no Christian perhaps is ever able to consider without some effort, feeling that he thereby endangers either his reverence towards God, or his humility, but which the errors of this day, and the confident tone of their advocates, oblige us to dwell upon, lest truth should suffer by our silence. The heavenly gift of the Spirit fixes the eyes of our mind upon the divine author of our salvation. . .

And again:

> And if he has at times, for instance, amid trial or affliction, special visitations and comfortings from the Spirit, "plaints unutterable". . . and passing

> gleams of eternal election, and deep stirrings of wonder and thankfulness thence following, he thinks too reverently of "the secret of the Lord" to betray (as it were) his confidence and, by vaunting it to the world, to exaggerate it perchance into more than it was meant to convey. But he is silent, and ponders it as choice encouragement to his soul, meaning something, but he knows not how much.[13]

Newman concludes the sermon on "The Gift of the Spirit":

> For ourselves, in proportion as we realise that higher view of the subject, which we may humbly trust is the true one, let us be careful to act up to it. Let us adore the sacred presence within us with all fear and "rejoice with trembling". Let us offer up our best gifts to him who, instead of abhorring, has taken up his abode in these sinful hearts of ours. . . In this then consists our whole duty, first in contemplating Almighty God, as in heaven, so in our hearts and souls; and next, while we contemplate him, in acting towards him and for him in the works of every day. . .[14]

Then in the sermon on "Christian Nobleness":

> Religious men, knowing what great things have been done for them, cannot but grow greater in mind in consequence. We know how power and responsibility change men in matters of this world. They become more serious, more vigilant, more circumspect, more practical, more decisive; they fear to commit mistakes, yet they dare more, because they have a consciousness of liberty and of power, and an opportunity for great successes. And thus the Christian, even in the way of nature, without speaking of the influence of heavenly grace upon him, cannot but change from the state of children to that of men, when he understands his own privileges. The more he knows and fears the

> gift committed to him, so much the more reverent is he towards himself, as being put in charge with it.[15]

Again and again Newman tries to describe for us and enable us to realise this gift;

> The Holy Ghost, I have said, dwells in body and soul, as in a temple. Evil spirits indeed have power to possess sinners, but his indwelling is far more perfect; for he is all-knowing and omnipresent, he is able to search all our thoughts, and penetrate into every motive of the heart. Therefore, he pervades us (if it may so be said) as light pervades a building, or as a sweet perfume the folds of some honourable robe; so that, in Scripture language, we are said to be in him, and he in us. . . It is plain that such an inhabitation brings the Christian into a state altogether new and marvellous, far above the possession of mere gifts.[16]

At the new birth of baptism the Christian enters the kingdom of Christ. "By this new birth the divine shechinah is set up within him, pervading soul and body, separating him really, not only in name, from those who are not Christians, raising him in the scale of being, drawing and fostering into life whatever remains in him of a higher nature."[17] And again:

> If Christ is our sole hope, and Christ is given us by the Spirit, and the Spirit be an inward presence, our sole hope is in an inward change. As a light placed in a room pours out its rays on all sides, so the presence of the Holy Ghost imbues us with life, strength, holiness, love, acceptableness, righteousness. . . That divine influence, which has the fullness of Christ's grace to purify us, has also the power of Christ's blood to justify. Let us never lose sight of this great and simple view. . . Christ himself vouchsafes to repeat in each of us in figure and mystery all that he did and suffered in the flesh. He is formed in us, born in us, suffers

in us, rises again in us, lives in us. . . and this divine presence constitutes the title of each one of us to heaven. . .[18]

Newman loves to remind us that we are temples of God. "We are assured of some real though mystical fellowship with the Father, Son and Holy Spirit. . . so that both by a real presence in the soul, and by the fruits of grace, God is one with every believer, as in a consecrated temple." "We are not our own; we are bought with the blood of Christ; we are consecrated to be temples of the Holy Spirit, an unutterable privilege, which is weighty enough to sink us with shame at our unworthiness, did it not the while strengthen us by the aid it itself imparts, to bear its extreme costliness. May we live worthy of our calling."[19]

With the great and exacting privilege go reasons for confidence. "Christ bids us do nothing we cannot do. . . He gives us the gift of his Spirit, and then he says, 'What doth the Lord require of thee, but to do justly, and to love mercy, and walk humbly with thy God?' and is *this* grievous?

"He who obeys God conscientiously, and lives holily, forces all about him to believe and tremble before the unseen power of Christ. . . When St Peter's disciple, Ignatius, was brought before the Roman emperor, he called himself Theophorus; and when the emperor asked the feeble old man why he so called himself, Ignatius said that it was because he carried Christ in his breast."[20] "Christ within is stronger than the world around us, and will prevail."[21]

In a famous sermon, "Shrinking from Christ's Coming", Newman says: "If indeed we have habitually lived to the world, then truly it is natural we should attempt to fly from him whom we have pierced. . . But if we have lived, however imperfectly, yet habitually, in his fear, if we trust that his Spirit is in us, then we need not be ashamed before him. We shall come before him as we now come to pray—with profound abasement, with awe, with self-renunciation, still as relying upon the Spirit which he has given us."

At Christ's coming to judge the world, "God the Son is without, but God the Spirit is within—and when the Son asks, the Spirit will answer. That Spirit is vouchsafed to us here; and if we yield ourselves to his gracious influences. . . he will assuredly be still with us and give us confidence in the day of judgment."[22] But the great doctrine does not only concern individuals, it leads on to the Body of Christ, his Church, and "cannot fail to produce in us deeper and more reverent feelings towards it, as his especial dwelling place".[23]

This has already been mentioned and will be considered again. In the Church, since our Lord's return to heaven, we are united to all three divine persons: "We have lost the sensible and conscious perception of Christ; we cannot look on him, hear him, converse with him, follow him from place to place; but we enjoy the spiritual, immaterial, inward, mental, real sight and possession of him; a possession more real and more present than that which the apostles had in the days of his flesh, *because* it is spiritual, *because* it is invisible. We know that the closer any object of this world comes to us, the less we can contemplate it and comprehend it. Christ has come so close to us in the Christian Church (if I may so speak), that we cannot gaze on him or discern him. He enters into us, he claims and takes possession of his purchased inheritance. . . he makes us his members."

Nor has he merely come to us again in his Spirit:

> No one, doubtless, can deny this most gracious and consolatory truth, that the Holy Ghost is come; but why has he come? to supply Christ's absence, or to accomplish his presence? Surely to make him present. Let us not for a moment suppose that God the Holy Ghost comes in such

> sense that God the Son remains away. No, he has not so come that Christ does not come, but rather he comes that Christ may come in his coming. Through the Holy Ghost we have communion with the Father and Son. . . You will say, how can Christ be present to the Christian and in the Church, yet not be on earth, but on the right hand of God? I answer that the Christian Church is made up of souls, and how can any of us say where the soul is, simply and really?[24]

Here and elsewhere in his Anglican writings Newman speaks of the presence of each of the divine persons in the soul, but confines himself to repeating the pregnant language of Scripture, saying that to discriminate further is beyond our powers. Thus he says: "This inward presence is sometimes described as God's presence or indwelling; sometimes that of Father and Son; sometimes of the Holy Ghost; sometimes of Christ the incarnate Mediator; sometimes of God through the Spirit."[25]

From these contemplative truths, Newman draws active conclusions. He was a man of action with a constant urge to use his talents in God's service. From Thomas Scott he had learned the watchwords "Holiness before peace", and "Growth the only evidence of life".[26] In the sermon "Sincerity and Hypocrisy" Newman asks:

> Are you living in the conviction of God's presence? And have you this special witness that that presence is really set up within you unto your salvation, namely that you live in the sense of it? Do you believe, and act on the belief, that his light penetrates and shines through your heart, as the sun's beams through a room? You know how things look when the sun's beams are on it. . . Let us then beg him to teach us the mystery of his presence in us, that, by acknowledging it, we may thereby possess it fruitfully. . . . In all circumstances of joy or sorrow, hope or fear, let us aim

> at having him in our inmost heart; let us have no secret apart from him. Let us acknowledge him as enthroned within us at the very springs of thought and affection. Let us submit ourselves to his guidance and sovereign direction; let us come to him that he may forgive us, cleanse us, guide us, and save us.[27]

The thought of the indwelling should make us watchful. It should also make us detached. It made Newman detached at Oxford, when so many cultivated and influential people were his disciples, and so many prizes lay at his feet. The Christian

> will be calm and collected under all circumstances; he will make light of injuries and forget them. . . And. . . on the other hand all this greatness of mind. . . which in other religious systems degenerates into pride, is in the Gospel compatible–nay rather intimately connected–with the deepest humility. . . Accordingly, the self-respect of the Christian is no personal and selfish feeling, but rather a principle of loyal devotion and reverence towards that Divine Master who condescends to visit him.[28]

And like the Master whom he possesses, he spends his life for others, he is another Christ.

Fortunately the Spirit of Christ comes invisibly: "It is in mercy that he hides himself from those who would be overcome by the sensible touch of the almighty hand. . . His visitation cannot but be awful anyhow, to creatures who know what we know, and are what we are. . . and though we joy, as well we may, yet we cannot joy with the light hearts of children, who live by sight, but with the thoughtful gladness of grown men."[29] Nevertheless the great privilege is a source of joy. The Holy Spirit "lives in the Christian's heart as a never-failing fount of charity. . . Where he is 'there is liberty' from the tyranny of sin. . .; doubt, gloom, impatience have been expelled;

joy in the Gospel has taken their place. . . How can charity towards men fail to follow?"[30] Elsewhere Newman asks what the doctrine is that will remove gloom and sorrow from Christians, and pour in light and joy:

> What but the great and high doctrine connected with the Church? They are not merely taken into covenant with God; they are taken into his Church. They have not merely the promise of grace; they have its presence... O fearful follower of Christ, how is it thou hast never thought of what thou art and what is in thee? . . . Much and rightly as thou thinkest of thy sins, hast thou no thought, I do not say of gratitude, but of wonder, of admiration, of amazement, of awful and overpowering transport, at what thou art through grace?[31]

Those are some of the passages in which Newman strove to show his audience the great pearl of the Gospel, and they cannot be better brought to an end than by his own conclusion to the sermon "The Gift of the Spirit":

> It were well if the views I have been setting before you, which in the main are, I trust, those of the Church Catholic from the beginning, were more understood and received among us. They would, under God's blessing, put a stop to much of the enthusiasm that prevails on all sides, while they might tend to dispel those cold and ordinary notions of religion which are the opposite extreme. Men of awakened and sensitive minds, knowing from scripture that the gift of the Holy Ghost is something great and unearthly, dissatisfied with the meagre notions of the many, yet not knowing where to look for what they need, are led to place the life of the Christian, which "is hid with Christ in God", in a sort of religious

> ecstasy, in a high-wrought sensibility on sacred subjects. . . and in an unnatural profession of all this in conversation. And further, from the same cause, their ignorance of the *supernatural* character of the Heavenly Gift, they attempt to measure it in each other by its sensible effects, and account none to be Christians but those whom they suppose they can ascertain to be such, by their profession, language and carriage. On the other hand, sensible and soberminded men, offended at such excesses, acquiesce in the notion, that the Gift of the Holy Ghost was almost peculiar to the apostles' day, that now, at least, it does nothing more than make us decent and orderly members of society. . . Such are the consequences which naturally follow, when, from one cause or other, any of those doctrines are obscured.[32]

It was partly with the idea of explaining various errors in the matter of grace, and showing how they could be reconciled in the higher doctrine of our personal union with an indwelling God, that Newman delivered in 1837 and published the following year, his *Lectures on Justification*. Père Bouyer has described them as "soaring above the unsatisfying aridities of text-book theology", and discovering "in the wealth of Catholic tradition the spirit that might have given those original Protestants complete satisfaction, fulfilling their aspirations and removing all risk of their falling into heresy or schism".[33]

Newman's aim was irenical and ecumenical. He wished to show that Catholic views and those of Protestants, except the extreme Evangelicals who held to a rigid doctrine of salvation by faith only, could be reconciled, not by an unsatisfactory compromise, but by a clearer and fuller understanding. Newman effected his purpose by an appeal to the doctrine of *gratia increata*, the presence of the indwelling God, as revealed in the New Testament. Protestants thought that the Catholic doctrine of grace fostered notions of human merit and was dangerous for the doctrine of justifying faith.

Having rejected Luther's explanation of justification, Christ's obedience imparted to us, as no answer, since the problem to be solved is not that of God's act in justifying, but the state of the justified person, Newman agrees that "to say with the Roman divines that justification consists in spiritual renovation, whether correct or incorrect, is perfectly intelligible. It is a real answer". Similarly, "the only serviceable answer on the Lutheran side is that justification consists in faith".[34]

But neither of these answers

> will be found to be sufficient and final. . . When faith is said to be the inward principle of acceptance, the question arises what gives to faith its acceptableness? faith is acceptable as having something in it which unbelief has not. . . It must be God's grace, if God's grace act *in* the soul, and not merely externally, as in the way of providence. If it acts in us, and has a presence in us when we have faith, then the having that grace or that presence, and not faith, which is its result, must be the real token, the real state of a justified man. Again, if we say that justification consists in a supernatural quality imparted to the soul, with the Roman writers. . . then. . . the question arises, is this quality all that is in us of heaven? does not grace itself, as an immediate divine power or presence, dwell in the hearts which are gifted with this renovating principle?

If so "then surely the possession of that grace is really our justification, and not renewal". "And thus," Newman concludes, "by tracing back farther the lines of thought on which these apparently discordant views are placed, they are made to converge, that is, supposing there to be vouchsafed to us an inward divine presence or grace, of which both faith and spiritual revnovation are fruits."[35] He then shows from the New Testament that what is there promised us is no mere quality of mind, but an inward gift, and reaches the triumphant conclusion: "*This* is to be justified, to receive the divine presence within us, and to be made a Temple of the Holy Ghost."[36]

Newman continues persuasively:

> We are told concerning mankind, that "in him we live, and move, and have our being". . . If this notion of the literal indwelling of God within us, whether in the way of nature or of grace, be decried as a sort of mysticism, I ask in reply whether it is not necessary truth that he is with us and in us, if he everywhere? And if he is everywhere and dwells in all, there is no antecendent objection against taking Scripture literally... that as he dwells in us in one mode in the way of nature, so he is in us in another in the way of grace.[37]

After all the New Testament texts, it is clear that "since this great gift is the possession of all Christians from the time they become Christians, justification. . . as certainly presupposes the gift, as the gift involves justification. In a word, what is it to have his presence within us, but to be his consecrated temple? What to be his temple, but to be set apart from a state of nature, from sin and Satan. . .? and what is this but to be justified?" Further, "whatever blessings in detail we ascribe to justification, are ascribed in Scripture to this sacred indwelling".[38]

The gift of the Spirit conveys the remission of our sins. Our adoption into the family of God is the work of the Spirit, whereby we say Abba, Father. Christ in us is our reconciliation with God and our life. Justification is said to lead to obedience; if we abide in Christ we bring forth much fruit. Christ "justifies us by entering into us, he continues to justify us by remaining in us. *This* is really and truly our justification, not faith, not holiness. . . but through God's mercy, the very presence of Christ."[39] This explains also the regeneration of infants: "For as God dwelt secretly in his material temple, ever hallowing it, yet only in season giving sensible evidence that he was there, so he may be present in their souls. . . without their being conscious or others witnesses of his work."[40]

The conclusion is that justification and renewal

> are both included in that one great gift of God, the indwelling of Christ in the Christian soul. . . It is the divine presence that justifies us, not faith, as say the Protestant schools, not renewal, as say the Roman. The word of justification is the substantive living Word of God, entering the soul, illuminating and cleansing it, as fire brightens and purifies material substances. He who justifies also sanctifies. . . the first blessing runs into the second. . . And the one cannot be separated from the other except in idea, unless the sun's rays can be separated from the sun, or the power of purifying from fire or water.[41]

The biblical and patristic revival in the Church have provided the solution to the problem, as one theologian puts it, "caused by an incorrect dualism between created and uncreated grace, as though they were separate things".[42] Matters were different when Newman was lecturing on justification, and changed little for a century. He reacted as we have reacted to the incomplete and distorted Catholic theology then prevalent. He thought unfortunate results flowed from the view that justification was renewal, to which Catholic writers thought they were committed by the Council of Trent.

Concentration on the idea of renewal suggests that all is a matter of good works and obedience, and men do not fix their "thoughts on Christ in that full and direct way of which Scripture sets the pattern".[43] "Hence the charge against Romanism, not unfounded as regards its popular teaching, that it views the influences of grace, not as the operations of a living God, but as something to bargain about and buy and traffic with."

Newman did not retract this as a Catholic, but merely added a note: "It requires a considerable acquaintance with the working of the Catholic system to have a right to speak of it."[44] He also said: "It is not nearly so consoling yet awful a doctrine to say, that we *have* had mercy and *shall* have reward. . . as to know, which I conceive is the full truth of the Gospel, that that perfection which is as yet but begun in our nature, is anticipated, pledged, and in one sense realised within us by a present gift."[45]

The scriptural and true Catholic view of justification, "fixes the mind, not on self but on Christ, and absorbs it in the vision of a present, and indwelling God". Newman ends, "When are we the more likely to dread sinning, when we know merely we ought to dread it, or when we see the exceeding peril of it? When are we the more likely to keep awake and be sober, when we have a present treasure now to lose, or a distant reward to gain?"[46] We have the great Gift partly now, fully hereafter.

From the New Testament doctrine that the Spirit is on earth because the Son is in heaven, it follows that at Pentecost the Holy Spirit was given not merely more abundantly than before, but, apart from exceptional cases, such as our Lady, for the first time. There is little about the Holy Spirit as sanctifier in the Old Testament, and St John is entirely in line with St Paul when he says, "as yet the Spirit was not given, because Jesus was not yet glorified".[47] This, as we know, was the teaching of the Greek Fathers to whom Newman was so devoted. The Holy Spirit was given dynamically in the Old Testament, substantially in the New. Newman points out that the indwelling was promised as the *distinguishing* grace of the Gospel. The same acceptableness before God can come in different ways, and what "at first sight seems a difficulty, that the attribute of righteousness, however conveyed to the old saints, should since Christ's coming be attendant on a divine gift, even his own sacred presence", is "an argument in favour of the doctrine. For such a transformation of shadows into substances, and human acts into divine endowments, far from being anomalous, is the very rule of the New Covenant."[48] Christ came, Newman points out, "to new-create—to begin a new line, and construct a new kingdom on the earth", "as the grace of the holy eucharist is the presence of Christ crucified, so the justification of those who approach it is the indwelling of Christ risen and glorified."[49]

Once more we see the emphasis on the relation with God as a personal one, not re-ified. Professor Gérard Philips, outlining how the treatise on grace ought to be written, insists that we must grasp the *religious* nature and *revealed* character of what is under discussion, and lays down: *"Incipiendum nobis erit a doctrina de gratia qualiter in Scriptura et Traditione antiqua proponitur, ne quidquam de ejus plenitudine et vitali virtute negligamus.*" And the same writer emphasises how in scripture our elevation by grace "*valde concrete et* **personalistice** *exprimitur*".[50]

We can thus see how authentic and balanced Newman's Anglican teaching was, and how masterly his grasp of revealed religion, years before he entered the Catholic Church. When he did so, he found theology at a low ebb; piety tended to be separate from it, and, although there were signs of hope, the standards, intellectual and spiritual, were uninspiring.

The sense of the indwelling of the Holy Spirit and through him of the Father and Son, had been Newman's support during the long agony of his Anglican deathbed. He had occasion to deal with the subject during those years, in the notes to his translation of St Athanasius. Throughout his Catholic life it remained his support. In the private retreat notes he made at Rome in 1847, before his Catholic ordination, he wrote: "I have not lost. . . my intimate sense of the divine presence in every place."[51]

At this time he was writing his novel *Loss and Gain*, and introduced into it his great ideal. The hero Charles is compared with his undergraduate friend, who became, not a Catholic, but the Fellow of a College. "Sheffield's whole heart was in his work, and religion was but a secondary matter to him. . . It was not the certainty of faith that made a sunshine to his soul. . . rather he had no perceptible need within him of that vision of the unseen which is the Christian's life." But "Charles' characteristic, perhaps above anything else, was an habitual sense of the divine presence; a sense of which, of course, did not ensure uninterrupted conformity of thought and deed to itself, but still there it was—the pillar of cloud before him and guiding him. He felt himself to be God's creature, and responsible to him—God's possession, not his own."[52]

On becoming a Catholic, however, Newman wrote little on the great subject. The atmosphere of the time was not propitious, and as a convert he did not wish to set up as a dogmatic and mystical teacher.

Nevertheless, in 1849 he did bring out a corrected Catholic edition of the fourth volume of *Parochial and Plain Sermons*. The alterations were made in deference to the strong advice he was given to do so. The new edition was a failure. People wanted Newman unexpurgated. Many years later the original volumes were reprinted. Something is to be learned from the alterations Newman thought it wise to make in the edition of 1849. A few were obvious ones: the distinction between mortal and venial sin was made clear, phrases such as "the Lord's table" were changed, and references to confession and the invocation of saints were introduced.

As to the doctrine of the indwelling, the great passages were still there. Newman retracts nothing of that, how could he? But in a few places there are curious tonings down, which suggest that he felt the teaching and language of scripture and the fathers were not altogether in tune with the prevailing fashion.

Thus, on p. 17, "Let us come to the ordinances of grace, in which Christ gives his Spirit" has been changed to "Let us come where he gives grace, let us come to his holy Church in which Christ vouchsafes to dwell." On p. 169, "He [Christ] came again in the person of his Spirit" is altered to "He gave them the gifts of the Spirit." On p. 229, "We have been brought into that mysterious presence of God which is in us and around us, and is in our heart", is changed to "brought under that mysterious power of God." On p. 247 Newman is speaking of those who came close to our Lord externally, his executioners, the beloved disciple. "His blessed Mother indeed came closer still to him; and we, if we be but true believers, still closer, who have him really though spiritually within us; but this is another, and inward sort of approach." Here the reference to the indwelling is removed, and the sense completely altered, no doubt to avoid any apparent slight to our Lady. It reads: "His blessed Mother, indeed, came closer still to him; but this is another, an inward sort of approach." Yet the Fathers praised our Lady because *prius concepit mente quam corpore*.[53] On p. 265, our Lord's presence in us by grace is turned into a reference to the blessed sacrament: "The presence of the eternal Son, ten times more glorious than when he trod the earth in our flesh, is with us", has become ". . . trod the earth, is in the sacred tabernacle still." Later writers have called attention to the danger of our being distracted from the real presence within us, which, as Newman often points out, the holy eucharist was supremely intended to subserve.

However, as has been said, great passages about the indwelling remained in this altered "Catholic" volume of *Parochial and Plain Sermons*. Newman never retracted. In 1874 he republished *Lectures on Justification*, with very few alterations–he called the Romanists more politely "the Roman divines"–and in a new preface wrote: "Unless the Author held in substance in 1874 what he published in 1838, he would not at this time be reprinting what he wrote as an Anglican."[54] In *Callista* the heroine turns over in her mind the impression St Cyprian and two other Christians had given her: "The three witnesses who had addressed her about Christianity had each of them made it consist in the intimate divine presence in the heart. It was the friendship and mutual love of person with person. Here was the very teaching demanded by her reason and her heart, which she found nowhere else."[55]

Towards the end of his life Newman had occasion to return to the great subject. Just when he received so unexpectedly and so providentially the cardinalate, he was engaged in preparing a new edition of *Select Treatises of St Athanasius*. The notes were now collected in a separate second volume, and thus became a collection of short essays on the main points of the theology of St Athanasius. In a dozen passages Newman speaks in scriptural and patristic language of the great privilege. Under the heading "Deification" he writes: "The titles which belong to the divine Word by nature, are by grace given to us, a wonderful privilege. . . The means by which these titles become ours are our real participation of the Son by his presence within us, a participation so intimate that in one sense he can be worshipped in us as being his shrine or temple. Athanasius insists on this doctrine again and again."[56]

The truth which the doctrine enshrines is the source of our prayer. We see how it entered into Newman's prayer from his posthumously published *Meditations and Devotions*. They show that one of the things which attracted Newman to St Philip was the latter's devotion to the Holy Spirit. Among Newman's meditations are the following: "My God, I adore thee, O Eternal Paraclete, the light and life of my soul. Thou mightest have been content with merely giving me good suggestions, inspiring grace and helping from without. . . But in thine infinite compassion thou hast from the first entered my soul, and taken possession of it. Thou hast made it thy temple."

And again: "O my God, can I sin when thou art so intimately with me? Can I forget who is with me, who is in me? Can I expel a divine inhabitant. . . My God, I have a double security against sinning; first the dread of such a profanation of all thou art to me in thy very presence; and next because I do trust that that presence will preserve me from sin."

Then the final prayer, for fervour: "Lord, in asking for fervour, I am asking for thyself, for nothing short of thee, O my God, who hast given thyself wholly to us. Enter my heart substantially and personally, and fill it with fervour by filling it with thee. Thou alone canst fill the soul of man, and thou hast promised to do so. Thou art the living flame, and ever burnest with love of man: enter into me and set me on fire after thy pattern and likeness."[57]

5 The world's benefactors

Whether he is considering the working of God in the natural world or in that of grace, Newman always draws attention to the hiddenness of his instruments. The factors that effect his providences are unconscious, and the personal influence of a few men is sufficient to carry on his noiseless work. The coming of God's kingdom is secret, because it is a conquest not of the body but of the heart. The weapons of its warfare were not carnal. "It came," says Newman, "by an inward and intimate visitation; by outward instruments, indeed, but with effects far higher than those instruments; with preaching and argument and discussion, but really by God's own agency. He who is omnipotent and omniscient touched many hearts at once and in many places."[1]

In his sermon for the feast of St Andrew, "The World's Benefactors", Newman maintains "that those men are not necessarily the most useful men in their generation, nor the most favoured by God, who make the most noise in the world, and who seem to be the principals in the great changes and events recorded in history". We must be on the look-out "for the true signs of God's presence, the graces of personal holiness manifested in his elect, which, weak as they may seem to mankind, are mighty through God, and have an influence upon the course of his providence, and bring about great events in the world at large, when the wisdom and strength of the natural man are of no avail".

And again:

> His marvellous providence works beneath a veil, which speaks but an untrue language; and to

> see him who is the truth and the life, we must stoop underneath it. . . Hid are the saints of God; if they are known to men, it is accidentally, in their temporal offices. . . To those who thus "follow on to know" him, he manifests himself, while he is hid from the world. They are near to him, as his confidential servants, and are the real agents in the various providences which occur in the history of nations, though overlooked by their annalists and sages.[2]

In one of his sermons preached in his University church at Dublin, Newman insists: "The kingdom of God spreads externally over the earth, because it has an internal hold upon us, because. . . it is within us, in the hearts of its individual members. Bystanders marvel; strangers try to analyse what it is that does the work; they imagine all manner of human reasons and natural causes to account for it."

And the Church herself is surprised. This was especially the case in the first three centuries, when abruptly "the overwheliming news was heard, that the Lord of the earth, the Roman Emperor had become a Christian, and all his multitude of nations with him. What an announcement! no human hand did it—no human instrument of it, preacher or apologist, can be pointed out. It was the secret power of God acting directly without observation upon the hearts of men."

And Newman continues: "That same marvel of an inward work in the souls of men on a large scale, which he wrought at first, he is ever reiterating and renewing in the history of the Church down to this day."

After instancing the revival after the collapse in the eighteenth century and the revolution, Newman gives the example of the Oxford Movement. "Those who fear the Church. . . those who never spoke to a Catholic priest, those who have never entered a Catholic church, those even who have learned their religion from the Protestant Bible, have, in matter of fact, by the over-ruling providence of God, been brought through that very reading to recognise the Mother of Saints."[3] Or as he wrote more pungently later, "Catholics did not make us Catholics; Oxford made us Catholics".[4] Newman brings his sermon to an end as follows:

> There are those who imagine that, when we use great words of the Church, invest her with heavenly privileges, and apply to her the evangelical promises, we speak merely of some external and political structure. They think we mean to spend our devotion upon a human cause, and that we toil for an object of human ambition. (E.g. party success or the praise of earthly superiors, and Newman had Archbishop Cullen in mind here!) But the text and train of thought I have been pursuing remind us of the true view of the matter, were we ever likely to forget it. The Church is a collection of souls, brought together in one by God's secret grace, though that grace comes to them through visible instruments, and unites them to a visible hierarchy. What is seen is not the whole of the Church, but the visible part of it. When we say that Christ loves the Church, we mean that he loves, nothing of earthly nature, but the fruit of his own grace—the varied fruits of his grace in innumerable hearts. . .[5]

In an early Oxford Movement sermon he had spoken of the Church as "all-glorious *within*, in that inward shrine, made up of faithful hearts, and inhabited by the Spirit of grace. We will put off, so be it, all secular, all political views of the victories of his kingdom. . . will not reckon on any visible fruit of our labour. We will be content to believe our cause triumphant, when we see it apparently defeated."[6]

These remarks are all the more striking when we remember that one of the chief purposes of the Movement was to defend the Church as a visible, hierarchical institution, with authority derived from the apostles. The early tracts had to insist that the Church was a visible body, and in his preaching Newman declares the word Church as "applied to the body of Christians in this world, means but one thing in Scripture, a visible body invested with invisible privileges".

And elsewhere:

> The visible Church of God is that one only company which Christians know as yet; it was set up at Pentecost, with the apostles for founders, their successors for rulers, and all professing Christian people for members. In this visible Church the Church invisible is gradually moulded and matured. Since this blessed consummation takes place in the unseen world, we may call it the invisible Church. Doubtless we may speak of the invisible Church in the sense of the Church in glory, or the Church in rest.[7]

Thus it was that on becoming a Catholic, Newman did not have to alter his idea of the Church, only recognise where the Church of the Fathers was now to be found. In fact he now attached much less importance to apostolic succession and to orders. With these in mind he wrote:

> Our starting point is not the fact of a faithful transmission of orders, but the standing fact of the Church, the visible and one Church, the reproduction and succession of herself from age to age. It is the Church herself that vouches for our orders, while she authenticates herself to be the Church not by our orders, but by her notes. It is the great note of an ever-enduring *coetus fidelium*, with a fixed organisation, a unity of jurisdiction, a political greatness, a continuity of existence in all places and times, a suitableness to all classes, ranks, and callings,

> an ever-energising life, an untiring, ever-evolving history, which is her evidence that she is the creation of God, and the representative and home of Christianity. She is not based upon her orders; she is not the subject of her instruments; they are not necessary for her idea. . . that ordinance is not simply of the essence of the Church; it is not more than an inseparable accident and a necessary instrument. Nor is the apostolic descent of her priests the direct warrant of their power in the eyes of the faithful; their warrant is her immediate, present, living authority; it is the word of the Church which marks them out as the ministers of God, not any historical or antiquarian research.[8]

Newman has also a great pragmatic argument for the Catholic Church, which he outlines in the *Apologia*. He asks: "What must be the face-to-face antagonist, by which to withstand and baffle the fierce energy of passion and the all-corroding, all-dissolving scepticism of the intellect in religious inquiries?. . . Things are tending. . . to atheism in one shape or other. What a scene, what a prospect does the whole of Europe present at this day!"[9]

That was in 1864! "Religious men, external to the Catholic Church, have attempted various expedients to arrest fierce, wilful human nature in its onward course, and to bring it into subjection. The necessity of some form of religion for the interests of humanity has been generally acknowledged. But where was the concrete representative of things invisible, which would have the force and the toughness necessary to be a breakwater against the deluge?"[10]

Newman proceeds to argue that there must be some guarantee, to preserve revealed religion from scepticism "in this anarchical world", some defence able to "make a stand against the wild living intellect of man." He concludes:

> Supposing then it to be the will of the creator to interfere in human affairs, and to make provision for preserving in the world a knowledge of himself, so definite and distinct as to be proof against the energy of human scepticism, in such a case. . . there is nothing to surprise the mind, if he should think fit to introduce a power into the world, invested with the prerogative of infallibility in religious matters. Such a provision would be a direct, immediate, active, and prompt means of withstanding the difficulty; it would be an instrument suited to the need; and, when I find that this is the very claim of the Catholic Church, not only do I feel no difficulty in admitting the idea, but there is a fitness in it which recommends it to my mind.[11]

Newman adds: "St Paul says in one place that his apostolical authority is given him to edification, and not to destruction. There could be no better account of the infallibility of the Church. Its object is, and its effect also, not to enfeeble the freedom or vigour of human thought in religious speculation, but to resist and control its extravagance."[12] Newman argued from a similar, although slightly different angle in *The Development of Doctrine*:

> The most obvious answer, then, to the question, why we yield to the authority of the Church in the questions and developments of faith, is that some authority there must be if there is a revelation given, and other authority there is none but she. A revelation is not given, if there be no authority to decide what it is that is given. In the words of St Peter to his Divine Master and Lord, "To whom shall we go?" Nor must it be forgotten in confirmation, that Scripture expressly calls the Church "the pillar and ground of truth", and promises her as by convenant that "the Spirit of the Lord shall be upon her".[13]

How has the Church managed to preserve the revelation in spite of the ravages of unbelief? Its authorities, popes and bishops played their part. As Newman said to Gladstone:

> Go through the long annals of church history, century after century, and say, was there ever a time when her bishops, and notably the Bishop of Rome, were slow to give their testimony on behalf of the moral and revealed law and to suffer for their obedience to it? ever a time when they forgot that they had a message to deliver to the world–not the task merely of administering spiritual consolation, or of making the sick-bed easy, or of training up good members of society, or of "serving tables" (though all this was included in their range of duty)–but specially and directly, a definite message to high and low, from the world's maker, whether men would hear or whether they would forbear?[14]

Yet Newman held most strongly that the Church was a communion, consisting of all her members. The bishops had their thrones in the Church of divine right and were the successors of the apostles, but he had no tendency to identify the Church with the hierarchy. It consisted of the whole people of God, of all those faithful people whose minds were enlightened by the Holy Spirit, whom they had received, and who were thus able to understand and preserve the revelation. The teaching was set forth in the creeds, but it was the personal possession of Christian minds, and was passed on from generation to generation. Newman's personalism and his sense of the Church as a body existing in history led him naturally to regard it in the first place as a communion. He remarked how, during the first three centuries,

> there was not one great mind, after the apostles, to teach and to mould her children. The highest intellects, Origen, Tertullian and Eusebius were

> representatives of a philosophy not hers; her greatest bishops, such as St Gregory, St Dionysius and St Cyprian, so little exercised a doctor's office, as to incur, however undeservedly, the imputation of doctrinal inaccuracy. Vigilant as was the holy see then. . . yet there is no pope, I may say, during that period, who has impressed his character upon his generation; yet how well instructed, how precisely informed, how self-possessed an oracle of truth, nevertheless, do we find the Church to be, when the great internal troubles of the fourth century required it. . . By what channels, then, had the divine philosophy descended down from the great teacher through three centuries of persecution? First, through the See and Church of Peter. . . but intercommunion was difficult, and comparatively rare in days like those, and of nothing is there less pretence of proof than that the holy see, while persecution raged, imposed a faith upon the ecumenical body. Rather, in that earliest age, it was simply the living myriads of the faithful, none of them known to fame, who received from the disciples of our Lord, and husbanded so well, and circulated so widely, and transmitted so faithfully, generation after generation, the once delivered apostolic faith; who held it with such sharpness of outline and explicitness of detail, as enabled even the unlearned instinctively to discriminate between truth and error, spontaneously to reject the very shadow of heresy, and to be proof against the fascination of the most luminous intellects, when they would lead them out of the narrow way.[15]

This point, that the faith is preserved by the faithful, was shown even more conclusively in the period after the Nicene Council, as Newman was to show in his famous article "On consulting the faithful in matters of doctrine":

> The Catholic people, in the length and breadth of

> Christendom, were the obstinate champions of Catholic truth, and the bishops were not. . . And again in speaking of the laity, I speak inclusively of their parish priests (so to call them), at least in many places; but on the whole, taking a wide view of the history, we are obliged to say that the governing body of the Church came short, and the governed were preeminent in faith, zeal, courage, and constancy. This is a remarkable fact; but there is a moral in it. Perhaps it was permitted in order to impress upon the Church. . . the great evangelical lesson that, not the wise and powerful, but the obscure, the unlearned, and the weak constitute her real strength. It was mainly by the faithful people that paganism was overthrown; it was by the faithful people, under the lead of Athanasius and the Egyptian bishops, and in some places supported by their bishops and priests, that the worst of heresies was withstood.[16]

Thus Newman maintained that at that time "the divine tradition committed to the infallible Church was proclaimed and maintained far more by the faithful than by the episcopate"; and "in that time of immense confusion the divine dogma of our Lord's divinity was proclaimed, enforced, maintained, and (humanly speaking) preserved, far more by the *Ecclesia docta* than by the *Ecclesia docens*; that the body of the episcopate was unfaithful to its commission, while the body of the laity was faithful to its baptism".[17] No wonder Père Bouyer can remark:

> It does not seem that any Catholic theology ever had gone so far, with such unerring discrimination, in affirming the active role of the whole body of the Church in the living custody of the faith. Few theologians, however, at that epoch, were prepared for the heart-rending reconsideration which this affirmation called for in certain presentations of the *Teaching Church* as opposed to the *Learning Church*. Did not these presentations arrive at the

> point of making two distinct Churches of them, one purely active, one purely passive, merely placed side by side?[18]

In an early sermon before the start of the Oxford Movement, Newman insisted that "the Christian Church is simply and literally a party or society instituted by Christ. He bade us keep together. Fellowship with each other, mutual sympathy, and what spectators from without call party-spirit, all this is a prescribed duty".[19]

At Oxford he had preached a spirituality for laymen, as a Catholic all his enterprises, those he succeeded in and those in which he was frustrated, were intended to serve and benefit them. He had so many lay friends, men and women, married and unmarried, and whole families. But if the laity were to do their work in the Church much was required of them.

> I want a laity, nor arrogant, not rash in speech, not disputatious, but men who know their religion, who enter into it. . . I want an intelligent, well-instructed laity. . . I wish you to enlarge your knowledge, to cultivate your reason, to get an insight into the relation of truth to truth, to learn to view things as they are. . . what are the bases and principles of Catholicism. . . I have no apprehension you will be the worse Catholics for familiarity with these subjects, provided you cherish a vivid sense of God above, and keep in mind that you have souls to be judged and saved. In all times the laity have been the measure of the Catholic spirit.[20]

Thus we return to the interiority of the Church, which has to withstand the fierce energy of passion and all-dissolving scepticism.

At the beginning of the Movement, too, he realised that the Church might have to *look to the people*. It could no longer depend on the state and the powerful.

> And what may become necessary in time to come,

> is a more religious state of things also. It will not be denied that, according to the Scripture view of the Church, though all are admitted into her pale, and the rich inclusively, yet the poor are her members with a peculiar suitableness and by a special right. Scripture is ever casting slurs upon wealth, and making much of poverty. "To the poor the Gospel is preached." "God has chosen the poor of this world, rich in faith and heirs to the kingdom." "If thou wilt be perfect, sell all that thou hast, and give to the poor." To this must be added the undeniable fact that the Church, when purest and when most powerful, *has* depended for its influence on its consideration by the many.[21]

In the *Apologia* Newman described his feelings on becoming a Catholic:

> I recognised at once a reality which was quite a new thing to me. Then I was sensible that I was not making for myself a church by an effort of thought; I needed not to make an act of faith in her. I had not painfully to force myself into a position, but my mind fell back upon itself in relaxation and peace, and I gazed at her almost passively as a great objective fact. I looked at her, at her rites, her ceremonial and her precepts, and I said, "This *is* a religion".[22]

Yet he knew always how weak the "concrete representative of things invisible"[23] was, even when regarded as a communion, to act as a breakwater against unbelief and heresy. When the Oxford Movement was at its height, he could still write:

> But in truth the whole course of Christianity from the first, when we come to examine it, is but one series of troubles and disorders. Every century is like every other, and to those who live in it seems worse than all times before it. The Church is ever ailing, and lingers on in weakness,

"always bearing about in the body the dying of the Lord Jesus, that the life also of Jesus might be made manifest in her body." Religion seems ever expiring, schism dominant, the light of truth dim, its adherents scattered. The cause of Christ is ever in its last agony, as though it were but a question of time whether it fails finally this day or another. The saints are ever all but failing from the earth, and Christ all but coming; and thus the day of judgment is literally ever at hand; and it is our duty to be ever looking out for it, not disappointed that we have so often said, "now is the moment", and that at the last, contrary to our expectation, truth has somewhat rallied. Such is God's will, gathering in his elect, first one and then another, by little and little, in the intervals of sunshine between storm and storm, or snatching them from the surge of evil, even when the waters rage most furiously. . . God alone knows the day and the hour when that will at length be, which he is ever threatening; meanwhile, thus much comfort do we gain from what has been hitherto—not to despond, not to be dismayed, not to be anxious at the troubles which encompass us. They have ever been; they ever shall be; they are our portion. "The floods are risen, the floods lift up their voice, the floods lift up their waves. The waves of the sea are mighty, and rage horribly; but yet the Lord who dwelleth on high, is mightier."[24]

Elsewhere Newman wrote:

The Church is ever militant; sometimes she gains, sometimes she loses; and more often she is at once gaining and losing in different parts of her territory. What is ecclesiastical history but the record of the ever-doubtful fortune of the battle, though its issue be not doubtful? Scarcely are we singing *Te Deum*, when we have to turn to our *Misereres*; scarcely are we at peace, when we are in persecution; scarcely have we gained a triumph,

> when we are visited by a scandal. Nay, we make progress by means of our reverses; our griefs are our consolations; we lose Stephen to gain Paul, and Matthias replaces the traitor Judas.[25]

Just as he was entering the Catholic Church he made this profession of faith, at the end of his book on development:

> It is true, there have been seasons when, from the operation of external or internal causes, the Church has been thrown into what was almost a state of *deliquium*; but her wonderful revivals, while the world was triumphing over her, is a further evidence of the absence of corruption in the system of doctrine and worship into which she has developed. If corruption be an incipient disorganisation, surely an abrupt and absolute recurrence to the former state of vigour, after an interval, is even less conceivable than a corruption that is permanent. Now this is the case with the revivals I speak of. After violent exertion men are exhausted and fall asleep; they awake the same as before, refreshed by the temporary cessation of their activity; and such has been the slumber and such the restoration of the Church. She pauses in her course, and almost suspends her functions; she rises again, and she is herself once more; all things are in their place and ready for action. Doctrine is where it was, and usage, and precedence and principle, and policy; there may be changes, but they are consolidations or adaptations; all is unequivocal and determinate, with an identity which there is no disputing. Indeed it is one of the most popular charges against the Catholic Church at this very time, that she is "incorrigible"– change she cannot, if we listen to St Athanasius or St Leo; change she never will, if we believe the controversialist or alarmist of the present day.[26]

From his earliest days at Oxford Newman realised that an intellectual movement was building up, which would sap the foundations of revealed religion. In his *University Sermons* he began to draw up a system of defence against it, which has already been mentioned. As long as he remained in Oxford, he held rationalism at bay, and Pusey deplored his departure, because "Newman, while he was with us, was its most powerful and successful antagonist".[27] As an old man, in the speech he made on receiving the cardinal's hat, he spoke of how he had spent his life fighting against the view that religious truth was unattainable, that is, liberalism in religion, which was spreading all over England. "I lament it deeply, because I foresee that it may be the ruin of many souls."

But he refused to lose confidence. "Christianity has been too often in what seemed deadly peril, that we should fear for it any new trial now. . . Commonly the Church has nothing more to do than to go on in her own proper duties, in confidence and peace; to stand still and see the salvation of God."[28]

Although Newman's serenity, based on the surest of all foundations, remained unshaken, yet he was filled with anguish at the thought of the trials he foresaw the generations after him would have to face. Occasionally he spoke with prophetic foresight of the calamitous visitations that lay ahead. Thus, just over a hundred years ago, he was asked to preach at the opening of a new seminary for the Catholic diocese of Birmingham, on 2 October 1873. He took as his theme the special peril of the times ahead, the spread of infidelity. This was what the seminarists he was addressing would have to face. He admitted that there were specific dangers to Christians at other times, which would not exist in the future, and continued: "Doubtless, but still, admitting this, I think that the trials which lie before us are such as would appal and make dizzy even such courageous hearts as St Athanasius, St Gregory I, or St Gregory VII. And they would confess that, dark as the prospect of their own day was to them severally, ours has a darkness different in kind from any that has been before it." Everything must now go by reason.

> There is no revelation from above. There is no exercise of faith. Seeing and proving is the only ground for believing. . . except in mathematics. . . truths are only probably such. So that faith is a mistake in two ways. First because it usurps the place of reason, and secondly because it implies an absolute assent to doctrines, and is dogmatic, which absolute assent is irrational. Accordingly you will find, certainly in the future, nay more, *even now, even now,* that the writers and thinkers of the day do not even believe there is a God. They do not believe either the *object*—a God personal, a providence, and a moral governor; and secondly, what they *do* believe, namely that there is some first cause or other, they do not believe with faith, absolutely, but as a probability.

Newman goes on: "You will say that their theories have been in the world and are no new thing. No. Individuals have put them forth, but they have not been current and popular ideas. Christianity has never yet had experience of a world simply irreligious." The ancient world of Greece and Rome was full of superstition but not of infidelity. They believed in the moral governance of the world. "Their first principles were the same as ours." And Newman points out how St Paul could appeal at Athens to the Unknown God, and speak to the people of Lystra of the living God who did them good from heaven. "And so when the northern barbarians came down at a later age, they, amid all their superstitions, were believers in an unknown providence and in the moral law. But we are now coming to a time when the world does not acknowledge our first principles."

Of course there would always be the faithful remnant, the seven thousand who had not bowed the knee to Baal, but as to the mass of people, Newman told his audience, "you are coming into a world such as priests never came into before."

A hundred years later, we have to admit that Newman's prophecy has been strikingly fulfilled. What was his remedy? While "every Catholic should have an intelligent appreciation of his religion. . . still controversy is not the instrument by which the world is to be resisted and overcome". We must remind ourselves of what we are as Christians, "a chosen generation, a kingly priesthood, a holy nation, a purchased people", words addressed to all Christians, and which belong especially ecclesiastics. And Newman proceeds to single out, as following from those words, one particular attitude,

> a spirit of seriousness or recollection. We must gain the habit of feeling that we are in God's presence, that he sees what we are doing; and a liking that he does so, a love of knowing it, a delight in the reflection, "Thou God seest me." A priest who feels this deeply will never misbehave himself in mixed society. It will keep him from over-familiarity with any of his people; it will keep him from too many words, from imprudent or unwise speaking; it will teach him to rule his thoughts. It will be a principle of detachement between him and even his own people; for he who is accustomed to lean on the unseen God, will never be able really to attach himself to any of his creatures. And thus an elevation of mind will be created, which is the true weapon which he must use against the infidelity of the world.[29]

Newman's remedy, then, is that we should try to live the highest truths of our faith. We should attend to the presence of our unseen God. No wonder Newman's favourite and often quoted text about the Church was that in the Epistle to the Hebrews: "But you have come to Mount Zion and to the city of the living God, the heavenly Jerusalem, and to unnumerable angels, in festal gathering and to the assembly of the first-born who are enrolled in heaven, and to a judge who is God of all, and to the spirits of just men made perfect, and to Jesus, the mediator of a new covenant"(*12:22, RSV*).

Nevertheless Newman had no illusions about the Catholic Church. He knew how much it stood in need of reform. In one of the last articles he wrote in defence of Anglicanism, he had this criticism to make:

> In antiquity, the main aspect of the economy of redemption comprises Christ, the Son of God, the author and dispenser of all grace and pardon, the Church his living representative, the sacraments her instruments, bishops her rulers, their collective decisions her voice, and Scripture her standard of truth. In the Roman schools we find St Mary and the saints the prominent objects of regard and dispensers of mercy, purgatory or else indulgences the means of obtaining it, the Pope the ruler and teacher of the Church, and miracles the warrant of doctrine. As to the doctrines of Christ's merits and eternal life and death, these points are not denied (God forbid!) but taken for granted and passed by in order to make way for others of more present, pressing and lively interest. That a certain change, then, in objective and external religion has come over the Latin, nay, and in a measure the Greek Church, we consider to be a plain historical fact; a change not indeed so great as is common Protestantism. . . but a change sufficiently startling to recall to our minds, with very unpleasant sensations, the words of the apostle, about preaching any other Gospel besides that which has been received.[30]

As a Catholic Newman would not allow these accusations, but we have to admit that they are not entirely without foundation. The invocation of saints, indulgences, the sacrificial aspect of the Mass, the hierarchical nature of the Church, and the juridical aspect were exaggerated, the great truths about the hidden divine element in the Church, the risen Christ and his presence in all believers, left on one side. There was an imbalance, which Newman who had derived such a balanced Catholicism from Scripture and the fathers tried to correct.

This explains why the reforming council, Vatican II, is so often described as "Newman's Council". He was ready to make excuses. "What has power to stir holy and refined souls is potent also with the multitude; and the religion of the multitude is ever vulgar and abnormal; it will ever be tinctured with fanaticism and superstition, while men are what they are. A people's religion is ever a corrupt religion, in spite of the provisions of Holy Church."[31]

However, writing in 1878, when the ultramontanes were triumphing, he had sorrowfully to admit, "It is so ordered on high that in our day holy Church should present just that aspect to my countrymen which is most consonant with their ingrained prejudice against her, most unpromising for their conversion."[32] Earlier he had written privately about his activity during his Catholic life:

> To me conversion was not the first thing, but the edification of Catholics. So much have I fixed on the latter as my object, that up to this time the world persists in saying that I recommend Protestants not to become Catholics. And, when I have given as my true opinion, that I am afraid to make hasty converts of educated men, lest they should not have counted the cost, and should have difficulties after they have entered the Church, I do but imply the same thing, that the Church must be prepared for converts, as well as converts prepared for the Church.[33]

There could hardly be a clearer statement of the ecumenical purpose of Newman's efforts to raise the level of their religion among Catholics.

As regards exaggerated devotion to the blessed Virgin Newman tells us in the *Apologia* about passages he found in some Italian authors: "Such devotional manifestations in honour of our Lady have been my great *crux* as regards Catholicism; I say frankly I do not fully enter into them now; I trust I do not love her less because I cannot enter into them".[34] This love needs no proving. Even as an Anglican Newman had a real devotion to our Lady, but it was based on revealed doctrine about her. As he wrote to Pusey in his *Letter* on the subject, "Though I hold, as you know, a process of development in apostolic truth as time goes on, such development does not supersede the fathers, but explains and completes them. And in particular, as regards our teaching concerning the blessed Virgin, with the fathers I am content. . . I do not wish to say more than they suggest to me, and I will not say less."[35] Already in *The Development of Doctrine* he had said: "It must be observed, what is very important, that great and constant as is the devotion which the Catholic pays to the blessed Mary, it has a special province, and has far more connection with the public services and the festive aspect of Christianity, and with certain extraordinary offices which she holds, than with what is strictly personal and primary in religion."[36] And in the *Apologia*, after saying that some Italian devotions were not suitable for England, and were not in the tradition of English Catholics, he went on:

> But, over and above England, my own case was special; from a boy I had been led to consider that my maker and I, his creature, were the two beings, luminously such *in rerum natura*. I will not here speculate, however, about my own feel-

> ings. Only this I know full well now, and did not know then, that the Catholic Church allows no image of any sort, material or immaterial, no dogmatic symbol, no rite, no sacrament, no saint, nor even the blessed Virgin herself, to come between the soul and its creator. It is face to face *solus cum solo*, in all matters between man and his God. He alone creates; he alone has redeemed; before his awful eyes we go in death; in his vision is our eternal beatitude.[37]

Newman made the point once more, and as strongly, in the *Letter to Pusey*. When our Lord became man,

> he brought home to us his incommunicable attributes with a distinctiveness which precludes the possibility of our lowering him merely by our exalting a creature. He alone has an entrance into our soul, reads our secret thoughts, speaks to our hearts, applies to us spiritual pardon and strength. On him we solely depend. He alone is our inward life; he not only regenerates us, but. . . he is ever renewing our new birth and our heavenly sonship . . . Mary is only our mother by divine appointment. . . her presence is above, not on earth; her office is external to us. Her name is not heard in the administration of the sacraments. Her work is not one of ministration towards us; her power is indirect. It is her prayers that avail, and her prayers are effectual by the *fiat* of him who is our all in all. Nor need she hear us by any innate power, or any personal gift; but by a manifestation to her of the prayers we make to her. . . and thus it is the divine presence which is the intermediating power by which we reach her and she reaches us.[38]

Newman holds in balance the greatness and the weakness of the Church. His programme remained what he described at the beginning of the Oxford Movement:

> We will unlearn, as sober and serious men, the expectation of any public displays of God's glory in the edification of his Church, seeing she is all-glorious *within*, in that inward shrine, made up of faithful hearts, and inhabited by the Spirit of grace. We will put off, so be it, all secular, all political views of the victories of his kingdom. . . we will not reckon on any visible fruit of our labour. We will be content to believe our cause triumphant, when we see it apparently defeated. . . We will work with zeal, but as to the Lord and not to men; recollecting that even apostles saw the sins of the churches they planted.[39]

Newman had plenty of experience of these sins as found in the Catholic Church, scholastic narrowness, superstition, intrigue and delations, the "aggressive insolent faction" of Ultramontanes, the "nihilism" which prohibited instead of creating and leading. He discussed the problem in the long preface of 1877 for the Catholic edition of his *Via Media*, showing how the Church, as representing Christ, shares, in human measure, his triple office of prophet, priest and king. She must give theological teaching, she must worship, and she must govern. The first tends to rationalism, the second to superstition and the third to ambition and tyranny. Newman insists that theology is the regulating principle, because it "is commensurate with revelation, and revelation is the initial and essential idea of Christianity".[40]

In this preface and elswhere Newman adumbrated a theology of abuses in the Church. The preface has been discussed by John Coulson and by Nédoncelle in a comprehensive article. Since then the full-scale treatise by Richard Bergeron, *Les abus de l'Eglise d'après Newman* (1971) has appeared. There has been no proper treatment yet of the freedom and free discussion in the Church, which Newman thought of such importance, as the final chapter of the *Apologia* emphasises.[41]

As to how reform was to be carried out, Newman infinitely preferred the way of St Philip to the way of Savonarola. In the sermon on "The Mission of St Philip" he says: "Savonarola, in spite of his personal sanctity, in spite of his protests against a mere external sanctity in Catholics, after all began with an external reform; he burned lutes and guitars, looking-glasses and masks, books and pictures, in the public square; but Philip bore with every outside extravagance in those whom he addressed, as far as it was not directly sinful, knowing well that if the heart was once set right, the appropriate demeanour would follow." And again, "Savonarola is associated in our minds with the pulpit rather than the confessional; his vehemence converted many, but frightened or irritated more. . . Philip had no vocation and little affection for the pulpit. . . He allured men to the service of God so dexterously, and with such a holy, winning art, that those who saw it cried out, astonished: 'Father Philip draws souls as the magnet draws iron.'"[41]

It was personal influence rather than new structures. As Newman said elsewhere of St Philip, "He preferred to yield to the stream and direct the current, which he could not stop, of science, literature, art, and fashion, and to sweeten and sanctify what God had made very good and man had spoilt." He added, "whether or not I can do anything at all in St Philip's way, at least I can do nothing in any other".[42]

Newman, then, saw the Church in all her deficiencies, with the eye of faith. The Holy Spirit was her life and her soul. Christ comes to it through his Spirit. It is taken up into the life of the Holy Trinity. "Thus the heart of every Christian," he says, "ought to represent in miniature the Catholic Church, since one Spirit makes both the whole Church and every member of it to be his temple."[43] But there is no undue individualism. We are sons together with Christ, *filii in Filio* (sons in the Son).

We are grafted invisibly into the body of Christ. In *Lectures on Justification* Newman describes in surprisingly modern terms how Christ's body has become the life of the Church. "The divine life which raised him, flowed over, and availed unto our rising again from sin and condemnation. It wrought a change in his sacred manhood, which became spiritual, without ceasing to be man, and was in a wonderful way imparted to us as a new-creating, transforming power in our hearts. This was the gift bestowed on the Church upon his ascension." Then, "He became a lifegiving Spirit, in the power of his Spirit he came to us, to justify us as he had been justified."[44]

6 The absolute claims of God

"Thou has made us for thyself, and our heart is restless till it rest in thee." Newman's sermon, "The thought of God the stay of the soul", is his commentary on these famous words. He begins by insisting "that the happiness of the soul consists in the exercise of the affections; not in sensual pleasures, not in activity, not in excitement, not in self esteem, not in the consciousness of power, not in knowledge; in none of these things lies our happiness, but in our affections being elicited, employed, supplied. . . Our true and real bliss lies in the possession of those objects on which our hearts may rest and be satisfied."[1] Newman concludes that

> the thought of God and nothing short of it is the happiness of man; for though there is much besides to serve as subject of knowledge, or motive for action, or means of excitement, yet the affections require a something more vast and more enduring than anything created. . . He alone is sufficient for the heart who made it. I do not say, of course, that nothing short of the Almighty Creator can awaken and answer to our love, reverence and trust; man can do this for man. Man doubtless is an object to rouse his brother's love, and repays it in his measure. Nay, it is a great duty, one of the two chief duties of religion, thus to be minded towards our neighbour. But. . . our hearts require something more permanent and uniform than man can be. We gain much for a time from fellowship with each other. It is a relief to us, as fresh air to the fainting, or meat and drink to the hungry, or a flood of tears to the

> heavy in mind. It is a soothing comfort to have those whom we may make our confidants. . . Love of home and family in these and other ways is sufficient to make this life tolerable to the multitude of men, which otherwise it would not be; but still after all, our affections exceed such exercise of them, and demand what is more stable. Do not all men die? are they not taken from us?

But, Newman continues,

> There is another reason why God alone is the happiness of our souls, to which I wish rather to direct our attention: the contemplation of him, and nothing but it, is able fully to open and relieve the mind, to unlock, occupy, and fix our affections. We may indeed love things created with great intenseness, but such affection, when disjoined from the love of the Creator, is like a stream running in a narrow channel, impetuous, vehement, turbid. The heart runs out, as it were, only at one door; it is not an expanding of the whole man. Created natures cannot open us, or elicit the ten thousand mental senses which belong to us, and through which we really live. None but the presence of our Maker can enter us; for to none besides can the whole heart in all its thoughts and feelings be unlocked and subjected.

Then Newman quotes the texts, "Behold I stand at the door and knock; if any man hear my voice and open the door, I will come in to him, and will sup with him, and he with me." "My Father will love him, and we will come unto him, and make our abode with him." "God hath sent forth the Spirit of his Son into your hearts." The conclusion is: "It is this feeling of simple and absolute confidence and communion, which soothes and satisfies those to whom it is vouchsafed." "The consciousness of a perfect and enduring presence, and it alone, keeps the heart open."[2]

This love is the peace of a good conscience, the

habitual consciousness that our hearts are open to God, the happiness that follows on repentance. It is also "that satisfaction and rest which the soul experiences in proportion as it is able to surrender itself wholly to God, and to have no desire, no aim, but to please him." There lie true affection and joy. Then the contrast:

> Many a great man, many a peasant, many a busy man, lives and dies with closed heart, with affections undeveloped, unexercised. You see the poor man, passing day after day, year after year, Sunday after Sunday, without a thought in his mind, to all appearance like a stone. You see the educated man, full of thought, full of intelligence, full of action, but still with a stone heart, as cold and dead as regards his affections, as if he were the poor ignorant countryman. You see others with warm affections, perhaps, for their families, with benevolent feelings towards their fellowmen, yet stopping there; centering their hearts on what is sure to fail them, as being perishable. Life passes, riches fly away, popularity is fickle, the sense decay, the world changes, friends die. One alone is constant; one alone is true to us; one alone can be true; one alone can be all things to us; one alone can supply our needs.

And Newman ends with the psalmist, "Whom have I in heaven but thee? and there is none on earth I desire in comparison with thee."[3]

In the sermon on equanimity Newman draws the further conclusion that joy and gladness are the characteristics of the Christian. He knows Christ's cause will triumph, and so he does not fear. "Fear is what makes men bigots, tyrants and zealots."[4] But there is a holy fear, which makes Christian joy sober and reverent. However, Newman insists, "Gloom is no Christian temper; that repentance is not real, which has not love in it; that self-chastisement is not acceptable, which is not sweetened by faith and cheerfulness. We must live in sunshine, even when in sorrow; we must live in God's presence, we must not shut ourselves up in our own hearts, even when we are reckoning up our past sins."[5]

Newman returns to the equanimity of the saints, and how their tribulations do not reach their depths. "The foundations of the ocean, the vast realms of water which girdle the earth, are as tranquil and as silent in the storm as in the calm. So it is with the souls of holy men. They have a well of peace springing up within them, unfathomable; and though the accidents of the hour may make them seem agitated, yet in their hearts they are not so." This is the underlying serenity which one can sense in Newman's life. He continues:

> The Christian has a deep, silent, hidden peace, which the world sees not. . . He is the greater part of the time by himself, and when he is in solitude, that is his real state. What he is when left to himself and to his God, that is his true life. He can bear himself; he can (as it were) joy in himself, for it is the grace of God within him, it is the presence of the eternal comforter in which he joys. He can bear, he finds it pleasant, to be with himself at all times, "never less alone than when alone". He can lay his head on his pillow at night, and own in God's sight, with overflowing heart, that he wants nothing–that he "is full and abounds"–that God has been all things to him, and that nothing is not his which God could give him. More thankfulness, more holiness, more of heaven he needs, indeed, but the thought that he can have more is not a thought of trouble, but of joy.

Newman ends with a definition:

> The Christian is cheerful, easy, kind, gentle, courteous, candid, unassuming; has no pretence, no affectation, no ambition, no singularity; because he has neither hope nor fear about this world. He is serious, sober, discreet, grave, moderate, mild,

> with so little that is unusual or striking in his bearing, that he may easily be taken at first sight for an ordinary man. There are persons who think religion consists in ecstasies, or in set speeches; he is not one of those.[6]

Finally, in the sermon "Love the one thing needful", Newman shows how love, and love only, is the fulfilling of the law. He quotes St Paul: "Though I speak with the tongues of men and angels and know all mysteries." "Spiritual discernment, an insight into the gospel covenant, is no evidence of love." Then "A tender consideration of the temporal wants of our brethren is another striking feature of St Paul's character, as it is a special characteristic of every true Christian; yet he says, 'Though I bestow all my goods to feed the poor, and have not charity, it profiteth me nothing.' Self-denying almsgiving is no necessary evidence of love."

Further, "although our Lord said 'If you love me, keep my commandments', yet love is not proportionate to obedience. . . It is possible to obey, not from love towards God and man, but from a sort of conscientiousness short of love; from some notion of acting up to a *law*; that is more from the fear of God than from love of him." That is the attitude of many, even religious people. They have their hearts set on the world, and are only restrained by rules. Outward lip service is paid to the claims of God. How are these evils to be remedied? This is Newman's cure:

> I must say plainly this, that, fanciful though it may appear at first sight to say so, the comforts of life are the main cause of it; and, much as we may lament and struggle against it, till we learn to dispense with them in good measure, we shall not overcome it. Till we, in a certain sense, detach ourselves from our bodies, our minds will not be in a state to receive divine impressions, and to exert heavenly aspirations. A smooth and easy life

> an uninterrupted enjoyment of the goods of providence, full meals, soft raiment, well-furnished homes, the pleasures of sense, the feeling of security, the consciousness of wealth—these and the like, if we are not careful, choke up all the avenues of the soul through which the light and breath of heaven might come to us.

Then, thinking perhaps of certain evangelicals of his day, Newman added: "If we attempt to force our minds into a loving and devotional temper, without this preparation, it is too plain what will follow: the grossness and coarseness, the affectation, the effeminacy, the unreality, the presumption, the hollowness. . . in a word, what scripture calls the hypocrisy, which we see around us."[7] He concludes: "After enjoining this habitual preparation of heart, let me bid you cherish, what otherwise it were shocking to attempt, a constant sense of the love of your Lord and Saviour in dying on the cross for you. . . Christ showed his love in deed, not in word, and you will be touched by the thought of his cross far more by bearing it after him than by glowing accounts of it."[8]

With the psychological insight he shows in his sermons, Newman has much to say on the ascetical preparation for the love of God. He exposes, as has been mentioned, the hypocrisy of apparently religious people, and has probing things to say on self-deceit and secret faults, and he popularised in English for the self-denial of the Christian, the use of the word "detachment".

> A great saint, St Philip Neri, said that if he had a dozen really detached men, he should be able to convert the world. To be detached is to be loosened from every tie which binds the soul to the earth, to be dependent on nothing sublunary, to lean on nothing temporal; it is to care simply nothing what other men choose to think or say of us, or do to us; to go about our own work, because it is our duty, as soldiers go to battle,

> without a care for the consequences; to account credit, honour, name, easy circumstances, comfort, human affections, just nothing at all, when any religious obligation involves the sacrifice of them.[9]

A word more frequently used by Newman for the ascetical preparation for union is surrender to God.

> What then is it that we who profess religion lack? ... It is this: a willingness to *be* changed, a willingness to suffer... almighty God to change us. We do not like to let go our old selves... We do not like to be new-made... But when a man comes to God to be saved, then, I say, the essence of true conversion is a *surrender* of himself, an unreserved, unconditional surrender; and this is a saying which most men who come to God cannot receive. They wish to be saved, but in their own way; they wish (as it were) to capitulate on terms, to carry off their goods with them; whereas the true spirit of faith leads a man to look off from self to God, to think nothing of his own wishes, his present habits, his importance or dignity, his rights, his opinions, but to say, "I put myself into thy hands, O Lord; make thou me what thou wilt; I forget myself... I will follow thee." In St Paul's words, "Lord, what wilt thou have me to do?" Here is the very voice of self-surrender.[10]

This, of course, is elementary Christian teaching, which any true pastor must put before his people, but it is worth while pausing to reflect once more how balanced Newman's presentation is. God indeed must be all in all, but this does not lead to a narrow other-worldliness. We have only to open *The Idea of a University* to realise this. Its purpose is "the enlargement of mind"; and "the culture of the intellect is a good in itself and its own end".

> The general culture of the mind is the best aid to professional and scientific study; and educated

> men can do what the illiterate cannot. . . A University training is the great ordinary means to a great but ordinary end. It aims at raising the intellectual tone of society, at cultivating the public mind, at purifying the national taste. . . It is education which gives a man a clear and conscious view of his own opinions and judgments, a truth in developing them, an eloquence in expressing them, and a force in urging them. It teaches him to see things as they are, to go right to the point, to disentangle a skein of thought, to detect what is sophistical, and to discard what is irrelevant. It prepares him to fill any post with credit, to master any subject with facility.[11]

Perhaps even more striking for our present purpose is Newman's account of marriage and celibacy, given in the sermon at the profession of a nun, the daughter of his first Oxford friend, John William Bowden. This is the description of marriage:

> Two mortal creatures of God, placed in this rough world, exposed to its many fortunes, destined to suffering and death, join hands, and give faith to each other that each of them will love the other wholly until death. Henceforth each is made for the other, each has possession of the affections of the other in a transcendent way; each loves the other better than anything else in the way; each is all in all to the other. . . Such is the fountainhead of society and the continual provision of the human race. . .

Newman then goes on to say that the gospel recommends celibacy, but "draws around it the choicest blessings of human nature, while it seems to be giving them up". On the other hand there is a state of celibacy, recommended by heathen philosophers, which only hardens the heart. They have praised and even observed celibacy, on the ground that it was higher than the common life of man. As to this Newman remarks: "To make a single life its own end, to adopt it simply and solely for its own sake, I do not know whether such a state of life is more melancholy or more unamiable, melancholy from its unrequited desolateness, and unamiable from the pride and self-esteem on which it is based. It is like a Mahometan's God, who from eternity has had no exercise of love." This is not the virginity of the gospel, which is a marriage with Christ. "The very idea of matrimony is possession—whole possession—the husband is the wife's and no other's, and the wife is the husband's and none but his. . . And this is to be married to Jesus. It is to have him ours wholly, henceforth and for ever."[12]

It would be easy to multiply examples of Newman's Christian humanism, and appreciation of the social virtues, but we must not forget his true sense of values in these matters. He insisted on the radical difference between mental refinement and genuine religion. There may be severe limitations in the hatred and disgust which a cultivated mind feels for some kinds of vice, and its humiliation at falling into them.

> Now this feeling may have its roots in faith and love, but it may not; there is nothing really religious in it, considered by itself. Conscience indeed is implanted in the breast by nature, but it inflicts upon us fear as well as shame. When the mind is simply angry with itself and nothing more, surely the true import of the voice of nature and the depth of its intimations have been forgotten, and a false philosophy has misinterpreted emotions which ought to lead to God. . . Fear carries us out of ourselves, whereas shame may act upon us only within the round of our own thoughts. Such, I say, is the danger which awaits a civilised age; such is the besetting. . . the ordinary sin of the intellect; conscience tends to become what is called a moral sense; the command of duty is a sort of taste; sin is not an

offence against God, but against human nature.

Thus, "Conscience has become self-respect. When such men do wrong, they feel not contrition of which God is the object, but remorse and a sense of degradation. They call themselves fools, not sinners; they are angry and impatient, not humble. . . *they are victims of an intense self-contemplation.*"[13]

Newman will have none of that. "Why is the framework of civilised society all so graceful and so correct? Why, on the other hand, is there so much of emotion, so much of conflicting and alternating feeling, so much that is high, so much that is abased, in the devotion of Christianity? It is because the Christian. . . has a revelation of God. . . he knows that one alone is holy. . . he knows that there is one to whom he owes everything."[14]

In order to make clear the absolute claims of God, which the civilised world was forgetting, and has forgotten more and more, Newman made two statements in his Lectures of 1850, which have always caused anger and astonishment. Montalembert was so delighted with them that he wrote to congratulate Newman on saying what so needed saying. The first one ran:

> The Church aims, not at making a show, but at doing a work. She regards this world, and all that is in it, as a mere shadow, as dust and ashes, compared with the value of a single soul. She holds that, unless she can, in her own way, do good to souls, it is no use her doing anything; she holds that it were better for sun and moon to drop from heaven, for the earth to fail, and for all the many millions who are upon it to die of starvation in extremest agony, so far as temporal affliction goes, than that one soul, I will not say, should be lost, but should commit one single venial sin, should tell one wilful untruth, though it harmed no one, or steal one poor farthing without excuse. She considers the action of this world and the

> action of the soul simply incommensurate, viewed in their respective spheres; she would rather save the soul of one single wild bandit of Calabria, or whining beggar of Palermo, than draw a hundred lines of railroad through the length and breadth of Italy, or carry out a sanitary reform, in its fullest details, in every city of Sicily, except in so far as these great national works tended to some spiritual good beyond them.

The other passage was this:

> The Church pronounces the momentary wish, if conscious and deliberate, that another should be struck down dead, or suffer any other grievous misfortune, as a blacker sin than a passionate, unpremeditated attack on the life of the sovereign. She considers direct unequivocal consent, though as quick as thought, to a single unchaste desire as infinitely more heinous than any lie that can possibly be fancied, that is, when that lie is viewed, of course, in itself, and apart from its causes, motives, and consequences. Take a mere beggar-woman, lazy, ragged and filthy, and not over-scrupulous of truth—I do not say she had arrived at perfection—but if she is chaste and sober and cheerful, and goes to her religious duties (and I am supposing not at all an impossible case), she will, in the eyes of the Church, have a prospect of heaven, which is quite closed and refused to the state's pattern-man, the just, the upright, the generous, the honourable, the conscientious, if he be all this, not from a supernatural power—I do not determine whether this is likely to be the fact, but I am contrasting views and principles—not from a supernatural power, but from mere natural virtue. Polished, delicate-minded ladies, with little of temptation around them, and no self-denial to practise, in spite of their refinement and taste, if they be nothing more, are objects of less interest to her, than

> many a poor outcast who sins, repents, and is with difficulty kept just within the territory of grace.[15]

In a letter of 1874, in defence of these arresting statements, Newman wrote: "I have contrasted virtue without the grace of God with virtue with it—and said that no merely natural virtue will be rewarded with heaven any more than beauty of person or high intellectual powers." He added:

> I suppose cleanliness of person is a sure and easy way to eternal life, and dirt is an absolute disqualification, in spite of what our Lord says of the "cup and platter" and of washing of hands before a meal. I suppose a soldier may be saved who has nothing more than the virtues of a soldier, a merchant who has nothing more than the mercantile virtues, a statesman with nothing more than political virtues, that an heroic Alexander the Great, that a large-minded, magnamimous Caesar, has achieved his salvation, when scripture says, "By grace ye are saved, through faith."[16]

And so we return to our theme. God has made us for himself, only he can satisfy us, he lifts us up to himself already in this world, and we must surrender to him. Thus, in spite of his humanism and his appreciation of the goodness in the world God has made, Newman is always bringing before us the opposition between the world and the Christian, between its standards and those of Christ. One of the lessons he learned from the Calvinist books at the time of his first conversion was what he calls in the *Apologia* the "main Catholic doctrine of the warfare between the city of God and the powers of darkness", and this was deeply impressed on his mind. He continually warns us against the world in this bad sense.

> Bad as it is to be languid and indifferent in our secular duties, and to account this religion, yet it

> is far worse to be the slaves of this world, and to have our hearts in the concerns of this world. I do not know anything more dreadful than a state of mind which is, perhaps, the characteristic of this country, and which the prosperity of this country so miserably fosters. I mean that. . . low ambition which sets everyone on the look-out to succeed and to rise in life, to amass money, to gain power . . . an intense, sleepless, restless, never-wearied, never satisfied, pursuit of mammon, to the exclusion of all deep, all holy, all calm, all reverent thoughts.[17]

Or again:

> What will it avail us then, to have devised some subtle argument, or to have led some brilliant attack, or to have mapped out the field of history, or to have numbered and sorted the weapons of controversy, and to have the homage of friends and the respect of the world for our successes—what will it avail to have had a position, to have followed out a work, to have reanimated an idea, to have made a cause triumph, if after all we have not the light of faith to guide us on from this world to the next.[18]

Then to the men of this world, "Prayer again is a mere indolence. It is better, they say, to put the shoulder to the wheel, than to spend time in wishing it to move. Again, making a stand for particular doctrines is thought unnecessary and unmeaning, as if there were any excellence or merit in believing this rather than that." Newman admits:

> God has graciously willed to bring us to heaven; to practise a heavenly life on earth certainly is a thing above earth. It is like trying to execute some high and refined harmony on an insignificant instrument. In attempting it, that instrument would be taxed beyond its powers, and would be sacrificed to great ideas beyond itself. And so, in

> a certain sense, this life, and our present nature, is sacrificed for heaven and the new creature; that while our outward man perishes, our inward man may be renewed day by day.[19]

The true Christian of primitive times was one who waited and watched for Christ. This separated him from the world.

> This is the very definition of a Christian—one who looks for Christ; not who looks for gain, or distinction, or power, or pleasure or comfort, but who looks "for the Saviour, the Lord Jesus Christ". This, according to Scripture, is the essential mark, this is the foundation of a Christian, from which everything else follows; whether he is rich or poor, high or low, is a further matter, which may be considered apart; but he surely is a primitive Christian, and he only, who has no aim of this world, who has no wish to be other in this world than he is; whose thoughts and aims have relation to the unseen; who has lost his taste for this world, sweet and bitter being the same to him. . . . There was no barrier, no cloud, no earthy object interposed between the soul of the primitive Christian and its saviour and redeemer. Christ was in his heart, and therefore all that came from his heart, his thoughts, words, deeds, and actions, savoured of Christ. . . The Christians of the New Testament had desired to sacrifice the kingdom of the world and all its pomps for the love of Christ, whom they had seen, whom they loved, in whom they believed. . .

And Newman concludes with an explanation of the prayer which our Lord had taught them:

> We often hear it said that the true way of serving God is to serve man, as if religion consisted merely in acting well our part in this life, not in direct faith, obedience and worship. How different is the spirit of this prayer! Evil round about him,

> enemies and persecutors in his path, temptation in prospect, help for the day, sin to be expiated, God's will in his heart, God's name on his lips, God's kingdom in his hopes: this is the view it gives us of a Christian.[20]

"God's kingdom in his hopes." He has made us for himself, the thought of him is our stay, Newman brought vividly before his generation, and brings before us still that unseen world where he dwells. The famous German Newmanist, Eric Przywara called Newman "the peculiar and unique *Augustinus redivivus* of modern times, and that because his gaze is calmly fixed upon the God of the end".[21] With the liturgy, we are to live in the thought of Christ's second coming. In the sermon entitled simply "Watching", Newman says:

> True Christians, whoever they are, watch, and inconsistent Christians do not. Now what is watching?. . . Do you know the feeling in matters of this life, of expecting a friend, expecting him to come, and he delays? Do you know what it is to be in unpleasant company, and to wish for the time to pass away, and the hour to strike when you may be at liberty? Do you know what it is to be in anxiety lest something should happen which may happen or may not, or to be in suspense about some important event, which makes your heart beat when you are reminded of it, and of which you think the first thing in the morning?. . Do you know what it is so to live upon a person who is present with you, that your eyes follow him, that you read his soul. . . that you anticipate his wishes? To watch for Christ is a feeling such as all these; as far as feelings of this world are fit to shadow out those of another.
>
> He watches for Christ who has a sensitive, eager, apprehensive mind; who is awake, alive, quick-sighted, zealous in honouring him; who looks out for him in all that happens, and who would not

> be surprised, who would not be over-agitated or overwhelmed, if he found that he was coming at once.
>
> And he watches *with* Christ, who, while he looks on the future, looks back on the past, and does not so contemplate what his Saviour has purchased for him as to forget what he has suffered for him . . . This then is to watch; to be detached from what is present, and to love in what is unseen; to live in the thought of Christ as he came once, and as he will come again; to desire his second coming, from our affectionate and grateful remembrance of his first.[22]

Newman is thus led to bring strikingly before us the Church in its eschatological aspect. The visible Church on earth is only a portion of the Church, preparatory for the Church of the elect, perfected and at rest. This idea is quite foreign to the world, which walks by sight and not by faith:

> The world then makes *itself* the standard of perfection and the centre of all good; and when the souls of Christians pass from it into the place of spirits, it fancies that this is *their* loss, not its own; it pities them in its way of speaking. . . Such is its opinion of the departed; as though *we* were in light and *they* in darkness, we in power and influence, they in weakness, we the living, and they the dead; yet with the views opened on us in the Gospel, with the knowledge that the one Spirit of Christ ever abides, and that those who are made one with him are never parted from him, and that those who die in him are irrevocably knit into him and one with him, shall we dare to think slightly of these indefectible members of Christ?. . . Shall we presume to compare that great assemblage of the elect, perfected and at rest, shall we weigh in the balance that glorious Church invisible, so populous in souls, so pure from sin. . . with ourselves, poor strugglers. . . whose names are not

> so written in the heavens, but they may be blotted out again? Shall we doubt for a moment, though St Paul was martyred centuries upon centuries since, that he... is present in the Church still, more truly alive than those who are called living?...[23]

As to our judgment, Newman saw it in the light of the truth that had come to him at his first conversion as a boy. In one of his last Anglican sermons he said:

> Earth must fade away from our eyes, and we must anticipate that great and solemn truth, which we shall not fully understand until we stand before God in judgment, that to us there are but two beings in the whole world, God and ourselves. The sympathy of others, the pleasant voice, the glad eye, the smiling countenance, the thrilling heart, which at present are our very life, all will be away from us, when Christ comes in judgment. Every one will have to think of himself. . . every one will be rendering to him his own account. By self-restraint, by abstinence, by prayer, by meditation, by recollection, by penance, we now anticipate in our measure that dreadful season. By thinking of it beforehand we hope to mitigate its terrors when it comes. By humbling ourselves now, we hope to escape humiliation then. . . We prepare to meet our God. . . We leave the goods of earth before they leave us.[24]

Newman was full of the realisation that his soul was naked before God, and God's utter purity. He was not afraid to speak of sin and its punishment.

What does he say of eternal punishment? One of the secrets of Newman's influence was his ability to enter into the minds of others, to understand the strength of a point of view which he did not share, and to meet it as far as he could. These characteristics may be seen in his treatment of the doctrine of eternal punishment, which, during the second half of his life, was increasingly denied. In 1849 he wrote in a letter, "about eternal punishment, it is to me, as to most men, the great crux in the Christian system as contemplated by the human mind. . . But then, *is there to be no trial of faith?*. . . Reason is able to approve of much–is it to approve of all?"[25]

The doctrine comes under faith, is to be accepted because it has been revealed. It comes at the end of a process. It is a fundamental thesis of Newman's that obedience to one's conscience, "a right state of heart", is what enables men to judge correctly in religious matters. Those in good moral dispositions are in the way to recognise the voice of the Good Shepherd. Having followed their inward guide, they realise that it is insufficient and are on the look-out for a revelation. This, says Newman, is why willingness to believe receives such praise in the Gospel. But once they have given their faith to Christ the revealer, they must accept all that Truth himself teaches. Thus Newman professes in the *Apologia*. "I believe the whole revealed dogma as taught by the apostles, as committed by the apostles to the Church, and as declared by the Church to me."Already, at the beginning of the same book, he tells us how, from his first conversion at the age of sixteen, "I have held with a full inward assent and belief the doctrine of eternal punishment, as delivered by our Lord himself, in as true a sense as I hold that of eternal happiness; though I have tried in various ways to make that truth less terrible to the imagination."[26] When as an old man Newman discussed the harm that would result from letting go the doctrine of eternal punishment, he began by avowing that he held the doctrine, "not because of the disintegrating consequences of letting it go, but on the simple word of the divine informant".

This was in an article of 1885, re-published in *Stray Essays*. After showing how the denial of the teaching of one part of holy Scripture would lead to the denial of other parts, Newman called attention to another disintegrating consequence, which was precisely the weakening of the natural conscience. Ordinary men may know that they should adhere to God with pure love, and yet welcome all that helps to keep them on the narrow path. As Newman puts it, "those solemn warnings of scripture against disobedience to the law of right and wrong are but fellows of the upbraidings and menaces of the human conscience. The belief in future punishment will not pass away without grave prejudice to that high monitor. Are you, in weakening its warning voice, to lose an ever-present reminder of an unseen God? It is a bad time to lose that voice when efforts so serious have so long been making to resolve it into some intellectual principle or secular motive."

A further disintegrating consequence is that Calvary, the work of our redemption, begins to lose its importance. Newman continues:

> but there is another doctrine, too, that suffers when future punishment is tampered with, namely, what is commonly called the "atonement". The divine victim took the place of man: how will this doctrine stand, if the final doom of the wicked is denied? Every one who escapes the penalty of pain, escapes it by virtue of the atonement made instead of it; but so great a price as was paid for the remission supposes an unimaginable debt. If the need was not immense, would such a sacrifice have been called for? Does not that sacrifice throw a fearful light upon the need of it? And if the need be denied, will not the sacrifice be unintelligible? The early martyrs give us their sense of it; they considered their torments as a deliverance from their full deserts, and felt that, had they recanted, it would have been at the risk of their eternal welfare. The great apostle is in his writings full of gratitude to the power who has "delivered him from the wrath to come".

> It is the foundation of the whole spiritual fabric on which his life is built. What remains of his Christianity if he is not longer to be penetrated by the thought of that second death from which he had been now delivered?[27]

So much as to the doctrine itself. How does Newman try to make it "less terrible to the imagination"? He begins, in *A Grammar of Assent* by insisting on the mystery. "The real mystery is, not that evil should never have an end, but that it should ever have had a beginning. Even a universal restitution could not undo what had been, or account for evil being the necessary condition of good. How are we to explain it, the existence of God being taken for granted, except by saying that another will, besides his, has had a part in the disposition of his work, that there is a quarrel without remedy, a chronic alienation, between God and man?" Newman insists that we ought,

> before we judge, to understand, not only the whole state of the case, but what is meant by the doctrine itself. Eternity, or endlessness, is in itself mainly a negative idea, though the idea of suffering is positive. Its fearful force, as an element of future punishment, lies in what it excludes; it means never any change of state, no annihilation or restoration; but what, considered positively, it adds to suffering, we do not know. For what we know, the suffering of one moment may in itself have no bearing, or but a partial bearing, on the suffering of the next; and thus, as far as its intensity is concerned, it may vary with every lost soul. This may be so, unless we assume that the suffering is necessarily attended by a consciousness of duration and succession, by a present imagination of its past and its future, by a sustaining power of realising its continuity.

In this view the fact of suffering, and its eternity, without a change of state, remain.[28]

Newman applied these same ideas in a letter as yet unpublished, of 1884.

> The only question is whether eternity of punishment is *in truth* inconsistent with the moral attributes of God. Before we say it is, we must know what eternity is. We only know the negative side, not the positive. "Punishment *never* ends." This proposition we *can* understand; but "punishment *ever* is"—this we *cannot* understand as a proposition. We cannot understand what eternity consists in, and in consequence we do not know what it adds, whether it adds any thing positive to the intensity of the punishment. For instance, whether *dates* be supposed to exist in eternity or not, it is plain how different time would be to what it is now, if it had not measurements. I say all this as suggesting the rashness of dogmatising on what is consistent with the divine attributes, and also what is not.[29]

Newman, however, refused to allow people merely to discuss the whole question in the abstract. The doctrine of eternal punishment was a concrete personal matter, which each individual must consider for himself and as applied to himself. Three years before the appearance of *A Grammar of Assent*, Newman wrote a vivid letter, again not yet published, to a lady who was troubled in her faith:

> *Can* you know about God's dealings with others, since *he* sees their hearts and you do not? But you can know something of his dealings with yourself. Now has he not ever been most loving and tender with you, and have you not been most ungrateful to him? What you *know*, is his dealings with *you*—what you *don't* understand, is his dealings with others. Go by what you know, instead of attempting what you don't know. Interpret what you don't know by what you do. Is it not hard that, for all his loving kindness to you, you

> will not trust him, you will not have faith in him, when he asks you by his own lips, for it is he who is the special herald of the awful doctrine of eternal punishment? What is meant by having faith, if you have nothing to try it? What *does* try it, what *do* we feel difficult to accept, but doctrines like this—which do not merely imply miracles, for miracles are mere contrarieties to nature, and God of course is the lord of nature, and can supersede what he has made—but which seem contrarieties in God himself?
>
> I grant that this doctrine seems to us inconsistent with his infinite love—but we cannot understand any of the divine attributes in their infinitude from the nature of the case—they run into mysteries—they seem to contradict each other. We cannot combine them. We understand enough of them to have ground for faith, hope and love towards him—and we must leave the difficulties which they involve when carried out to their perfection to be solved for us by himself in a higher state of being.

After putting forward the considerations about eternity described above, Newman concluded his letter:

> I discern clearly but one thing, viz. that the state of the lost is never reversed, that they never will see the face of God, or enter heaven, that they never will be annihilated, yet never be in company with the saints. These are awful *negatives*—but they are negatives which are inflicted on lost souls by themselves—for it would be but an increase of misery for an unholy soul to be brought into heaven, and it remains unholy by its own act. No positive pain is necessary for the fullness of the second death. Sinners are self condemned, self punished.[30]

Newman was more gentle and less personal with this lady, than he allowed St Cyprian to be with Callista: "'Nothing will ever make me believe that all my people have gone and will go to an eternal Tartarus.' 'Had we not better confine ourselves to something more specific, more tangible?' asked Caecilius, gravely. 'I suppose if one individual may have that terrible lot, another may—both may. Suppose I understand you to say that you never will believe that *you* will go to an eternal Tartarus.' Callista gave a slight start, and showed some uneasiness or displeasure. 'Is it not likely,' continued he, 'that you are better able to speak of yourself, and to form a judgment about yourself, than about others? Perhaps if you could first speak confidently about yourself, you would be in a better position to speak about others also'."[31]

As to Purgatory, Newman's teaching is that of St Catherine of Genoa, although he had not read her work. He showed its purificatory rather than its penal purpose. Instead of legal categories and satisfaction, Newman spoke of the holiness of God and the unworthiness of man. He describes the feeling of the loving soul as it approaches its judgment: "To see his face, though for a moment! to hear his voice, to hear him speak, though it be to punish! O Saviour of men, it says, I come to thee, though it be in order to be at once remanded from thee; I come to thee, who art my life and my all. . . I have seen this day thy face and it sufficeth. . ."[32]

This personal relationship between the loving soul and the all-holy God is brought out in *The Dream of Gerontius*. There the angel warns Gerontius that "the flame of everlasting love doth burn ere it transform", and explains:

> . . . thou wilt hate and loathe thyself; for, though
> Now sinless, thou wilt feel that thou has sinned,
> As never thou didst feel; and wilt desire
> To slink away, and hide thee from his sight;
> And yet wilt have a longing aye to dwell
> Within the beauty of his countenance
> And these two paths, so counter and so keen—

The longing for him, when thou seest him not;
The shame of self at thought of seeing him—
Will be thy veriest, sharpest purgatory.[33]

After the vision of his Saviour Gerontius cries:

Take me away, and in the lowest deep
There let me be
And there in hope the lone night-watches keep...
There will I sing my absent Lord and Love...
That sooner I may rise, and go above,
And see him in the truth of everlasting day.[34]

And what of the everlasting day? When Newman's sister died at the end of the year in which he became a cardinal, some of his family seem to have thought that in sending his condolences to her children, he had not spoken of the hope of being reunited to her. At any rate, he wrote to one of his nephews:

> Looking beyond this life, my first prayer, aim and hope is that I may see God. The thought of being blessed with the sight of earthly friends pales before that thought. I believe that I shall never die; this awful prospect would crush me, were it not that I trusted and prayed that it would be an eternity in God's presence. How is eternity a boon, unless he goes with it? And for others dear to me, my one prayer is that they may see God. It is the thought of God, his presence, his strength, which makes up, which repairs all bereavements... I prayed that it might be so, when I lost so many friends thirty-five years ago, what else could I look to?... I said Mass for your mother, it was to entreat the lover of souls that, in his own way and in his own time, he would remove all distance that lay between the sovereign good and her, his creature. That is the first prayer, *sine qua non*, introductory to all prayers, and the most absorbing.[35]

The first of Newman's published sermons bore the

title "Holiness necessary for future blessedness" and he showed how out of place the unbeliever, the sensual man would feel in heaven. It would be hell to an irreligious man. In the Church we are brought together and prepared for heaven. Already Christ provides a home for us where we may seek the creator. Characteristically, Newman's chief sermon on heaven is one on the subject of the Holy Trinity, "Peace in believing", on Father, Son and Holy Spirit, who abide in us.

> All God's providences, all God's dealings with us, all his judgments, mercies, warnings, deliverances, tend to peace and repose as their ultimate issue. All our troubles and pleasures here, all our anxieties, fears, doubts, difficulties, hopes, encouragements, afflictions, losses, attainments, tend this one way. . . after our soul's anxious travail; after the birth of the Spirit; after trial and temptation; after sorrow and pain, after daily dyings to the world; after daily risings unto holiness; at length comes the "rest which remaineth unto the people of God". After the fever of life; after wearinesses and sicknesses; fightings and despondings; languor and fretfulness; struggling and failing, struggling and succeeding; after all the changes and chances of this troubled unhealthy state, at length comes death, at length the white throne of God, at length the beatific vision. After restlessness comes rest, peace, joy—our eternal portion, if we be worthy—the sight of the blessed three, the holy one; the three that bear witness in heaven; in light unapproachable.[36]

Notes

1 Seeking the elusive truth

1. *G. A.* pp. 56-57: *An Essay in aid of a Grammar of Assent.*
2. *Apo.* p. 1: *Apologia pro Vita Sua.*
3. *Apo.* p. 3.
4. *A. W.* p. 169: JOHN HENRY NEWMAN, *Autobiographical Writings, ed.* Henry Tristram, 1956.
5. *Apo.* p. 4.
6. Cf. C. S. DESSAIN, "Cardinal Newman and the Doctrine of Uncreated Grace", in *The Clergy Review* 47 (1962) 207-225, 269-288;
7. *Apo.* pp. 4-6.
8. *Apo.* p. 4.
9. *A. W.* p. 63.
10. *A. W.* pp. 200-201.
11. Cf. C. S. DESSAIN, "Cardinal Newman and the Eastern Tradition", in *The Downside Review* no 315, April 1976, pp. 83-98.
12. R. W. CHURCH, *The Oxford Movement*, London 1892, pp. 21-22.
13. R. W. CHURCH, *Occasional Papers, II,* p. 457.
14. A. VONIER, *A Key to the Doctrine of the Eucharist*, chap. VIII, "Sacramental Harmony". *Collected Works* of Abbot Vonier, vol. 2, 1952, pp. 261-265.
15. See above, note 2.
16. *Apo.* p. 43.
17. WILLIAM LOCKHART, *Cardinal Newman*, London 1891, pp. 25-26.
18. Obituary notice in *The Guardian*, 13 August 1890. [Quoted in *The Correspondence of John Henry Newman with John Keble and Others* pp. 389-390.]
19. *A. W.* p. 249.
20. *Call.* p. 327: *Callista, A Tale of the Third Century.*
21. "They were a furious party who made a schism within the African Church, and not beyond its limits. It was a case of Altar against Altar, of two occupants of the same See. . . What a light was hereby thrown upon every controversy in the Church!. . . For a mere sentence, the words of St Augustine, struck me with a power which I never had felt from any words before." *Apo.* pp. 116-117.
22. *Apo.* p. 117.
23. The "Branch Theory" of the Church is thus summarised by Newman: "The Catholic Church in all lands had been one from the first century

for many centuries; then, various portions had followed their own way to the injury, but not to the destruction, whether of truth or of charity. These portions or branches were mainly three: the Greek, Latin, and Anglican. Each of these inherited the early undivided Church *in Solido* as its own possession. Each branch was identical with that early undivided Church, and in the unity of that Church it had unity with the other branches. . .", *Apo.* p. 70.

24. *Correspondence of John Henry Newman with John Keble and Others* 1839-1845, edited at the Birmingham Oratory, London 1917, p. 219.
25. *U. S.* p. 323: *Fifteen Sermons preached before the University of Oxford.*
26. *U. S.* p. 331.
27. "Dogmatic Constitution on Divine Revelation", Art 2. *Vatican II: The Conciliar and Post Conciliar Documents*, ed. A. Flannery 1975, p. 751 (slightly different wording: ". . . mediator and the sum total of Revelation.").
28. *Dev.* p. 89: *An essay on the Development of Christian Doctrine.*
29. [Unfortunately, this phrase has defied all attempts at identification. It resembles many phrases in the *Apologia* and *Difficulties of Anglicans*, vol. II. The only clue is in C. S. DESSAIN, *John Henry Newman*, p. 83, where it is quoted without the precise reference being given.]
30. *Correspondence of John Henry Newman with John Keble and Others* p. 351.
31. *Ibid.* p. 364.
32. *Apo.* p. 238.
33. *Newman the Oratorian* 1969, p. 62.
34. *L. D.* XI, p. 30: *Letters and Diaries.* Letter of 9 November 1845 to J. D. Dalgagairns.
35. *L. D.* XI, p. 306.
36. *L. D.* XI, p. II.
37. MERIOL TREVOR, *Newman Light in Winter* London 1962, p. 150.
38. *L. D.* XIX, p. 179.
39. *D. A.* p. 295: *Discussions and Arguments on Various Subjects.*
40. *Diff.* II, p. 24: *Certain Difficulties felt by Anglicans in Catholic Teaching.*
41. *U. S.* p. 259.
42. Cf. *Apo.* p. 116. Cf. also *L. D.* XXV, p. 95, Letter of 12 April 1870 to Robert Whitty.
43. *L. D.* XXIX, p. 195. Letter, 6 November 1879 from Octavius Ogle, son of an Anglican friend.
44. W. WARD, *The Life of John Henry Newman*, London 1913, vol. II, p. 527.
45. *Ibid.* p. 486.

2 Personal influence

1. *U. S.* Sermon V, pp. 75-98.
2. *Ibid.* p. 87.
3. *Ibid.* p. 91.
4. *Ibid.* p. 92.
5. *Ibid.* p. 93.

6. *Ibid.* p. 96.
7. *Idea* p. 409: *The Idea of a University defined and illustrated.*
8. *Apo.* p. 19.
9. *G. A.* pp. 220, 238.
10. *D. A.* pp. 364-5.
11. *Heb 11:6.*
12. *U. S.* p. 259.
13. *U. S.* p. 275.
14. *U. S.* p. 217.
15. *O. S.* p. 64: *Sermons preached on Various Occasions; G. A.* pp. 112, 104.
16. *O. S.* pp. 64-65.
17. *Call.* p. 314.
18. *O. S.* p. 65.
19. *O. S.* p. 66.
20. *O. S.* p. 74.
21. *Mix.* pp. 225-226: *Discourses addressed to Mixed Congregations.*
22. *Apo.* p. 241.
23. *U. S.* pp. 194-195.
24. *Idea* pp. 453-454.
25. *L. D.* XXV, p. 97.
26. *Call.* p. 293.
27. *P. S.* I, pp. 19-20: *Parochial and Plain Sermons.*
28. *Dialogues* Book 2, chap. 3. P. Lugano *(ed.), Sancti Benedicti Vita et Regula*, Paris, Desclée 1929, p. 11: "He dwelt alone, by himself, under the eyes of God looking at him from heaven."
29. *P. S.* III, pp. 116, 124.
30. *Ess.* II, pp. 190-192: *Essays Critical and Historical.*
31. *P. S.* IV, p. 261.
32. *H. S.* II, p. 94: *Historical Sketches.*
33. *P. S.* VIII, pp. 154, 165.
34. *O. S.* p. 114.
35. *P. S.* II, p. 53.
36. *P. S.* V, pp. 44-45.

3 Christ hidden

1. *Diff.* II, pp. 86-87.
2. *Dev.* pp. 324-326.
3. *P. S.* III, pp. 169-170.
4. *T. T.* pp. 167-168: *Tracts Theological and Ecclesiastical.*
5. *T. T.* pp. 170-171.
6. *T. T.* pp. 178-179.
7. *P. S.* VI, pp. 60-61.
8. VLADIMIR LOSSKY, *The Mystical Theology of the Eastern Church*, London 1973, pp. 149 and 243.

9. *P. S.* III, p. 170.
10. *Ath.* I, II, vol. II, pp. 327 and 426: *Select Treatises of St Athanasius.*
11. *T. T.* pp. 380-381.
12. *Ari.* p. 219: *The Arians of the Fourth Century.*
13. *The Quarterly Review* July 1883, pp. 381-382.
14. R. W. CHURCH, *The Oxford Movement*, pp. 191-192.
15. *P. S.* III, p. 130.
16. *P. S.* III, p. 166.
17. *P. S.* V, p. 118.
18. *M. D.* pp. 492, 493: *Meditations and Devotions of the late Cardinal Newman,* 2nd edn, 1893.
19. *Ath.* II, p. 43.
20. *Ari.* pp. 136 and 272.
21. *Ath.* II, pp. 92-93.
22. *Correspondence with John Keble and Others* London 1917, p. 206.
23. *Ess.* I, p. 66.
24. *Mix.* p. 307.
25. *Ess.* I, pp. 247-248.
26. *Ess.* I, p. 367.
27. *P. S.* IV, pp. 169-171.
28. *P. S.* II, pp. 144, 148.
29. *P. S.* VI, p. 136.
30. *P. S.* III, p. 277.
31. *P. S.* II, p. 91.
32. *P. S.* VII, p. 231.
33. *P. S.* III, p. 352.
34. *P. S.* II, p. 154.
35. *Ibid.* p. 155.
36. *P. S.* II, p. 227.
37. *Ath.* II, pp. 193-195.
38. *P. S.* V, p. 10.
39. *Diff.* I, p. 81.
40. *Call.* p. 221.
41. *M. D.* p. 512.
42. *Jfc.* p. 325: *Lectures on the Doctrine of Justification.*

4 The indwelling Spirit

1. *P. S.* III, p. 102.
2. *P. S.* VI, p. 123.
3. *P. S.* II, p. 221.
4. *Jfc.* p. 203.
5. *Ibid.* p. 205.
6. *Ibid.* pp. 206-207.
7. *Apo.* p. 5.

8. THOMAS SCOTT, *Essays on the Most Important Subjects in Religion*, (9th edn 1822), p. 169.
9. MS. Birmingham Oratory Archives.
10. Unpublished MS. Sermon on Prayer, 25 July 1824. (Birmingham Oratory Archives, A. 17.1, No. 5.) This forms part of a projected edition of Newman's unpublished Anglican sermons.
11. JOHN HENRY NEWMAN, *Autobiographical Writings* (1956), p. 169.
12. *U. S.* pp. 28-29 (uniform edition).
13. *P. S.* II, pp. 224 and 226.
14. *P. S.* III, p. 269.
15. *S. D.* p. 143: *Sermons bearing on Subjects of the Day.*
16. *P. S.* II, p. 222.
17. *P. S.* III, pp. 266-267.
18. *P. S.* V, pp. 138-140.
19. *P. S.* II, pp. 35 and 60.
20. *P. S.* I, pp. 106 and 292-293.
21. *P. S.* II, p. 150.
22. *P. S.* V, pp. 55-57.
23. *P. S.* III, p. 23.
24. *P. S.* VI, pp. 121-127.
25. *Jfc.* p. 150-151.
26. *Apo.* p. 5.
27. *P. S.* V, pp. 235-236.
28. *S. D.* pp. 144-148.
29. *S. D.* p. 139.
30. *P. S.* II, p. 230.
31. *P. S.* IV, pp. 145-146.
32. *P. S.* VII, pp. 268-269.
33. LOUIS BOUYER, *Newman, His Life and Spirituality*, p. 171.
34. *Jfc.* pp. 134-136.
35. *Jfc.* pp. 136-137.
36. *Jfc.* p. 144.
37. *Jfc.* pp. 144-145.
38. *Jfc.* p. 149.
39. *Jfc.* pp. 149-150.
40. *Jfc.* p. 152.
41. *Jfc.* p. 154.
42. G. PHILIPS, "De ratione instituendi tractatum de Gratia nostrae sanctificationis", in *Ephemerides Theologicae Lovanienses* (April-Sept. 1953), p. 357.
43. *Jfc.* p. 186.
44. *Ibid.*
45. *Jfc.* p. 188.
46. *Jfc.* pp. 190-191.
47. *John 7:39.*

48. *Jfc.* p. 193.
49. *Jfc.* pp. 194, 201.
50. "We must begin with the doctrine of grace as taught in Scripture and in the ancient tradition, lest we neglect anything of its fullness and living force expressed in a very concrete and personalist way." G. PHILIPS, *art. cit.* pp. 355-356.
51. *Autobiographical Writings* p. 247.
52. *L. G.* pp. 230-231: *Loss and Gain: the story of a Convert*
53. Cf. St Augustine, *Sermon 25*, 7-8: *The Divine Office*, III, p. 409. ". . . Christ the truth is in Mary's mind, Christ made flesh is in her womb. Greater is that which is in her mind than that which she carried in her womb."
54. *Jfc.* p. ix.
55. *Call.* p. 293.
56. *Ath.* II, p. 88.
57. *Meditations and Devotions* (2nd edn 1893), pp. 554, 555, 559.

5 The world's benefactors

1. *O. S.* p. 49.
2. *P. S.* II, pp. 4, 9, 11.
3. *O. S.* pp. 53-54.
4. *The Letters and Diaries of John Henry Newman* XIX, p. 352. (Letter of 2 June 1860 to E. E. Estcourt.)
5. *O. S.* pp. 56-57.
6. *P. S.* II, p. 93.
7. *P. S.* III, pp. 221, 240, 223.
8. *Ess.* II, pp. 88-89.
9. *Apo.* pp. 243-244.
10. *Ibid.* p. 244.
11. *Ibid.* p. 245.
12. *Ibid.* p. 253.
13. *Dev.* pp. 88-89.
14. *Diff.* II, p. 197.
15. *H. S.* I, p. 208.
16. *The Arians of the Fourth Century* pp. 445-446. J. COULSON *(ed.) On Consulting the Faithful in matters of Doctrine* 1961, pp. 109-110.
17. *Ibid.* p. 465.
18. *L'Eglise. . .* p. 143.
19. *P. S.* VII, p. 241.
20. *Prepos.* p. 390: *Lectures on the Present Position of Catholics in England.*
21. *H. S.* I, p. 341.
22. *Apo.* pp. 339-340.
23. *Apo.* p. 244.
24. *V. M.* I, pp. 354-355: *The Via Media of the Anglican Church.*
25. *H. S.* II, p. 1.

26. *Dev.* p. 444.
27. Letter to Dr Hook, 8 November 1846. Quoted in H. P. LIDDEN, *Life of Edward Bouverie Pusey, D. D.*, London 1894, vol. III, p. 116.
28. W. WARD, *The Life of John Henry Newman* II, p. 462.
29. *Catholic Sermons of Cardinal Newman* 1957, pp. 212, 123, 125, 132-3.
30. *Ess.* II, p. 8.
31. *Diff.* II, p. 80.
32. *V. M.* I, 3rd edn 1877, p. xxvii.
33. *Autobiographical Writings* p. 258.
34. *Apo.* p. 195.
35. *Diff.* II, p. 24.
36. *Dev.* p. 428.
37. *Apo.* p. 195.
38. *Diff.* II, p. 83.
39. *P. S.* II, p. 93.
40. *V. M.* I, p. xlvii.
41. C. S. DESSAIN, "Newman's Philosophy and Theology", in *Victorian Prose, A Guide to Research*, ed. D. J. DeLaura, New York 1973, p. 180.
42. *O. S.* pp. 236, 237.
43. *Idea* pp. 235, 238.
44. *S. D.* p. 132.
45. *Jfc.* pp. 207-208.

6 The absolute claims of God

1. *P. S.* V, pp. 315-316.
2. *Ibid.* pp. 316-319.
3. *Ibid.* pp. 325-326.
4. *P. S.* V, p. 65.
5. *P. S.* V, p. 271.
6. *P. S.* V, pp. 69-71.
7. *P. S.* V, pp. 329-331, 337-338.
8. *Ibid.* p. 338.
9. *H. S.* III, p. 130.
10. *P. S.* V, pp. 241-242.
11. *Idea* p. 177, 165, 178.
12. Newman's Oratory Papers No. 18, 12 January 1854: P. MURRAY, *Newman the Oratorian* Dublin 1969, pp. 275, 277.
13. *Idea* pp. 191, 192.
14. *O. S.* p. 27.
15. *Diff.* I, pp. 239, 249.
16. Letter of 15 October 1874 to Emily Bowles: *The Letters and Diaries of John Henry Newman* XXVII, pp. 137-138.
17. *Apo.* p. 6; *P. S.* VIII, p. 159.
18. *Mix.* pp. 191-192.

19. *S. D.* p. 87.
20. *S. D.* pp. 278, 279, 281, 287, 289.
21. E. PRZYWARA, "Saint Augustine and the Modern World": *A Monument to Saint Augustine: Essays on some Aspects of his Thought written in Commemoration of his 15th Centenary* London 1930, p. 286.
22. *P. S.* IV, pp. 322-325.
23. *P. S.* IV, pp. 178-179.
24. *S. D.* p. 38.
25. *L. D.* XIII, p. 318. Letter of 2 December 1849 (1963).
26. *Apo.* pp. 251-256. Uniform edition.
27. *S. E.* pp. 83-88: *Stray Essays on Controversial Points,* privately printed 1890. See also *The Theological Papers of John Henry Newman on Faith and Certainty* (ed. H. M. de Achaval and J. D. Holmes), O.U.P. 1976, pp. 146-149.
28. *G. A.* pp. 399, 422, 503. Newman explained to his nephew about the passage quoted: "What I meant to say was this, that there are needless *exaggerations*, made popularly, of a doctrine, grave enough in itself."
29. Letter of 12 December 1884.
30. Letter of 3 July 1867.
31. *Call.* pp. 216-217.
    In pp. 138-144 above is reproduced the essay by C. S. Dessain, *Cardinal Newman and Eternal Punishment* (Verlag Styria), pp. 715-719.
32. *Mix.* p. 81.
33. *Verses on Various Occasions* pp. 355-356.
34. *Ibid.* p. 362-363.
35. Letter of 26 February 1880: W. WARD, *The Life of Cardinal Newman* II, p. 479.
36. *P. S.* VI, p. 369.